SOUTH CYPRI GUIDE 2026

Uncover the Rich Heritage of the Mediterranean Paradise

Kenneth A. Patridge

Copyright © 2026

All rights reserved. No part of this publication may be reproduced, distributed, or transmitted in any form or by any means — electronic, mechanical, photocopying, recording, or otherwise — without the prior written permission of the author, except in the case of brief quotations used in reviews or articles.

SUN, STONE, AND SIMPLE JOY: WHY I WROTE THIS SOUTH CYPRUS GUIDE FOR YOU

I didn't mean to fall in love with South Cyprus. I thought I was coming for a quick break — a few beaches, a few ruins, back to real life. But the island had other plans.

On my first morning, I walked along a quiet stretch of sand where the sea looked like melted glass. A fisherman waved. I waved back and kept walking until my feet sank into warm water and tiny fish darted around my ankles. Later that day, I stood in front of ancient mosaics in Paphos, so bright it felt like the past hadn't gone anywhere at all. By sunset, I was on a cliff near Petra tou Romiou, watching the sky turn peach and gold. That was the moment I knew: I wasn't just visiting; I was connecting.

Of course, I also made every classic travel mistake. I picked a busy beach when there was a calmer one ten minutes away. I arrived at a monastery as the doors closed for the afternoon break. I circled the same roundabout twice while the GPS "recalculating…" mocked me in three languages. But each wrong turn unlocked a small win: a family-run taverna with grilled halloumi and lemon potatoes, a tiny church with cool stone and flickering candles, a backstreet bakery that put warm honey on loukoumades and refused to let me pay for the extra one they slipped into my bag.

I met people who made the island feel like a friend. A shop owner in Lefkara showed me lace patterns and told me, "Kopiaste — come in." A bus driver in Limassol pointed out where to hop off for the best beach walk. A grandma in Omodos pressed a glass of sweet Commandaria wine into my hand and said, "You'll like this," and she was right. Every day felt like another layer of the island opening up — beach days, mountain air, village squares, ancient stones, late-night music, and food that tastes like sunshine.

But here's the truth I learned the hard way: South Cyprus is easy to love and oddly tricky to plan. The island is packed with treasures, but not every treasure is on a clear sign. Some places are best at sunrise, some after 4 p.m., some only when the sea is calm. Some roads look fast and aren't. Some "must-sees" are skippable, while the small side-turn with no fancy name is the thing you'll remember forever.

That's why I wrote this book.

I wanted to make South Cyprus simple — for first-timers who don't know where to start, and for returning travelers who want to go deeper without the trial-and-error. I wrote down the things I wish I'd known: the beaches that stay calm when the wind picks up, the quiet coves near the busy bays, the short cuts through towns, the right side of the parking lot for a fast exit, the best times for Kourion's theater (hint: when the light gets soft), the easy route to the Blue Lagoon, the shady side of Avakas Gorge at midday, where to find local meze without a long wait, and how to line up a day so you're never rushing but always doing.

I tested every chapter with my own feet. I hiked the trails and counted the steps. I tried the buses and the boats and the back roads. I learned which flip-flops are fine and which paths need real shoes. I noted where the good coffee is near each site (because sometimes you need a freddo cappuccino before history). I mapped bathroom stops, picnic spots, shaded benches, and photo angles that don't look like everyone else's postcards.

This guide isn't just a list. It's a companion. It talks like a friend who knows your time is precious. It gives you choices: "Want easy and beautiful? Do this." "Want adventure? Try that." "Got kids?

Here's the path with shade and ice cream at the end." "Back for a second trip? Here are the places locals love but don't shout about."

I also share my small joys — the ones that made me feel at home here: the first bite of a citrusy village salad after a swim; fig tree shadows on white stone; the sound of church bells over the sea; the way the wind climbs the hills in the Troodos and smells like pine and sun-warmed rock. These details matter. They're why we travel — not just to see, but to feel.

If you're holding this book, I want you to feel calm before your plane even lands. I want you to flip to a page and know exactly where to go, when to go, how to go, and what to skip. I want you to get the big moments — the ruins, the cliffs, the bays — without the hassle. And I want you to get the little moments too — the smile from the baker, the last light on the water, the nap under an umbrella that turns a good day into a perfect one.

South Cyprus gave me more than a trip. It gave me a rhythm: slow mornings, bright afternoons, easy nights. It showed me that simple is not boring; simple is beautiful when it's done right. That's the heart of this guide — to make your journey smooth and rich, so you can spend less time figuring things out and more time falling in love.

So let's start. Pick a chapter. Pick a mood. I'll lead the way, step by sunny step. And by the end, I hope you'll say what I said as I watched another soft sunset slide into the sea: "I can't wait to come back."

Contents

SOUTH CYPRUS TRAVEL GUIDE 2026 1

Sun, Stone, and Simple Joy: Why I Wrote This South Cyprus Guide for You 3

Planning Your Trip 10

    Best Time To Visit 10

    Entry Requirements and Visa Information 12

    Currency and Banking 14

    Language and Communications 15

    Transportation: Getting Around 16

    Health and Safety 17

Cities & Regions Overview 18

    Nicosia: The Divided Capital 18

    Limassol: History Meets Modernity 20

    Larnaca: Coastal Charm and Culture 21

    Paphos: Ancient Ruins and Seaside Beauty 23

    Troodos Mountains: Nature and Adventure 25

    Ayia Napa And Protaras: Sun, Sand, and Nightlife 26

Must-See Attractions 28

    Nicosia 28

        Ledra Street and the Green Line 28

        The Selimiye Mosque (Cathedral of Saint Sophia) 30

        The Cyprus Museum 32

        Famagusta Gate 34

    The Venetian Walls and Bastions..36
Limassol...38
    The Kourion Archaeological Site..38
    The Amathus Ruins..40
    Limassol Castle and Medieval Museum......................................42
    Fasouri Watermania Waterpark..44
    Kolossi Castle..46
Larnaca..48
    Larnaca Salt Lake and Hala Sultan Tekke.................................48
    Larnaca Castle..50
    The Zenobia Wreck Dive Site...52
    Mackenzie Beach..54
    Choirokoitia Neolithic Settlement..56
Paphos..58
    Paphos Archaeological Park (Tombs of the Kings, House of Dionysos)..58
    Petra tou Romiou (Aphrodite's Rock)...60
    Aphrodite's Baths...62
    Akamas Peninsula and Blue Lagoon...64
Ayia Napa And Protaras..66
    Fig Tree Bay..66
    The Ayia Napa Monastery..68
    The Sculpture Park..70
    The Thalassa Museum...71

- The Underwater Sculpture Park 73
- Nissi Beach 74
- The Troodos Mountains 76
  - Kykkos Monastery 76
  - Mount Olympus 78
  - Omodos Village 80
  - Wine Villages and Vineyards 82
  - Caledonia and Millomeris Waterfalls 84
- Activities And Experiences 86
  - Water Sports and Diving 86
  - Hiking and Nature Trails 89
  - Wine Tasting and Vineyard Tours 92
  - Cultural Festivals and Events 95
  - Nightlife and Entertainment 99
  - Shopping: Markets and Boutiques 103
  - Culinary Delights: Where to Eat 107
  - Cycling Routes and Mountain Biking 110
  - Rock Climbing and Caving 114
  - Skiing and Snowboarding on Mount Olympus 118
  - Horseback Riding 121
  - Paragliding and Aerial Tours 124
- Hidden Gems And Off-the-Beaten-Path 127
  - Lefkara Village (Lace and Silver) 127
  - Agios Nikolaos tis Stegis Church 130

    Saint Hilarion Castle..132

    Avakas Gorge..135

    Linos tou Charilaou Wine Press... 137

Day Trips and Excursions..139

    Day Trip to the Akamas Peninsula.. 139

    Exploring the Karpas Peninsula.. 142

    Visit to the Troodos Mountains... 144

    Cultural Tour of Lefkara and Omodos..147

    Coastal Boat Tours and Cruises.. 150

ACCOMODATION... 152

    Hotel... 152

    Villas.. 155

    Guest Houses... 158

    Holiday Apartments...161

Practical Information.. 164

    Local Etiquette and Customs... 164

    Accessibility for Disabled Travelers..167

    Sustainable Travel Tips..170

    Shopping Hours and Public Holidays.......................................172

Conclusion.. 174

PLANNING YOUR TRIP

Best Time To Visit

Deciding when to visit South Cyprus can entirely shape your experience, as each season offers a completely different side of the island. You have the luxury of choosing what kind of holiday you want, whether it's a sun-soaked beach escape or a cool, quiet cultural journey.

If you are a lover of nature and the outdoors, then you will find that spring, which runs from March through May, is simply magical. This is when the entire island bursts into a carpet of vibrant wildflowers and the air is fresh and mild. The weather is perfect for hiking the trails of the Akamas Peninsula or exploring the ancient archaeological sites without the intense heat of summer. You will be able to enjoy the lush, green landscapes before they turn golden in the summer sun, making it an ideal time for photography and leisurely walks.

For those who dream of long, lazy days on the beach, summer, from June to August, is your ideal time. The sun shines brightly for hours, the sea is beautifully warm and inviting, and all the resorts and towns are buzzing with life. This is the peak season, so you can expect the beaches to be lively and the nightlife to be at its best. If you can handle the heat, which can get quite high, you will be rewarded with a holiday full of swimming, water sports, and unforgettable evenings spent dining al fresco by the sea.

If you prefer a balance of good weather and fewer crowds, then the autumn months of September and October are an excellent choice. The scorching summer heat has softened, but the sea remains wonderfully warm, so you can still enjoy swimming and sunbathing. This is a brilliant time for exploring the island's vineyards and tasting the famous Cypriot wines, as well as visiting historical sites in much more comfortable temperatures. The atmosphere is more relaxed, allowing you to get a real feel for local life.

At last, winter, from December to February, presents a serene and quiet side of South Cyprus. While you might experience some rain, the days are often still bright and mild, especially compared to much of Europe. This is the perfect season for a peaceful cultural escape, where you can explore museums, enjoy cozy tavernas, and have the ancient ruins almost all to yourself. It is also the only time you can experience the unique contrast of the island by heading up to the Troodos Mountains, where you can even go skiing on the snow-capped peaks.

Entry Requirements and Visa Information

Before you can feel the warm Cypriot sun on your skin, there's a small but important first chapter of your journey to write, and it all starts with your passport. As you hold it in your hand, you'll feel a sense of anticipation, but first, you need to make sure everything is in order.

Imagine that South Cyprus, as a member of the European Union, is like a familiar and welcoming home. For many of you traveling from other EU countries, this home opens its doors wide, and all you need is your passport or even just your national ID card. It's a simple, easy entry that lets your adventure begin the moment you land. There is a single, crucial detail to remember, however. While Cyprus is part of the European family, it hasn't yet joined the Schengen zone. This is actually a great thing for you, as it means your time here won't count against your travel days in places like France or Germany, giving you more freedom to explore.

For those of you traveling from places like the United States, the UK, Canada, or Australia, your passport is your golden ticket. You can typically arrive without a visa for a stay of up to ninety days, which gives you plenty of time to explore the entire island. Your passport just needs to be valid for a few months past your planned departure date, a small detail that ensures your journey is completely seamless. If your home country does require a visa, your adventure begins a little earlier with a visit to a Cypriot embassy to get your papers in order.

There is one final, essential rule of the road you need to know. The Republic of Cyprus considers the international airports in Larnaca and Paphos, and their main seaports, as the only legal gateways to the island. If you were to somehow arrive through an airport or port in the northern part of the island, it would be seen as an illegal entry by the authorities. This is a crucial piece of information to ensure you avoid any potential trouble and that your trip starts on the right foot. To make sure your story begins perfectly, your final act of preparation should be a quick double-check of the official government travel site to confirm all the rules, guaranteeing your wonderful adventure can start without a single worry.

Currency and Banking

When you are on the island, managing your money is a simple and straightforward affair. The official currency used everywhere in South Cyprus is the **Euro (€)**, so you will see all prices marked clearly with that symbol.

To make your trip as easy as possible, it is best to have a mix of payment options ready. You can rely on your credit and debit cards, especially **Visa** and **Mastercard**, for most of your larger purchases. They are widely accepted at hotels, big supermarkets, and major restaurants. However, you will quickly discover that cash is essential for the authentic, everyday experiences. You will need it for a coffee in a small, traditional cafe, for fresh produce at a local village market, or to pay for a taxi ride.

Finding cash is no trouble at all. You will see **ATMs** readily available in every city and in most towns, making it easy to withdraw money whenever you need it. Just be sure to check with your home bank before you travel to find out about any potential fees for using your card abroad.

Tipping is also a part of the culture here, but it is not as strict or formal as in some other countries. If you are happy with the service at a restaurant, it is customary to leave a small tip, usually around 10 percent of the bill. For a quick coffee or a small purchase, rounding up to the nearest Euro is a kind way to show your appreciation. Having a little bit of cash in your wallet ensures you are prepared for every situation and can enjoy your trip without a single worry.

Language and Communications

Navigating communication in South Cyprus is surprisingly easy, so you can feel completely at ease. The official language of the island is **Greek**, and you will see it used on all the street signs and menus. However, you'll quickly discover that you will have no trouble getting around because **English is very widely spoken**. Almost everyone working in the tourism industry—from hotel staff to waiters in restaurants and shopkeepers—speaks English fluently.

While you can comfortably get by with just English, making an effort to learn a few basic Greek words is a wonderful way to connect with the local people. Cypriots are known for their warmth, and they will appreciate your effort with a big smile. Try saying a simple "hello" with **yassas**, or "thank you" with **efcharisto**. If you need to say "please," it's **parakalo**, which can also mean "you're welcome." You will find that these small gestures can often lead to a much more genuine and friendly interaction.

Don't worry about mastering the pronunciation; the effort itself is what counts. You will find that people are happy to help you, and hand gestures or a simple point can work wonders if you find yourself in a more rural area where English might be less common. The key is to be open and friendly. Cypriots love to chat and share their culture, so a little bit of effort on your part will be rewarded with a very warm welcome.

Transportation: Getting Around

Once you are in South Cyprus, you will find that getting from one place to another is an adventure in itself, and you have several great options depending on your travel style. The most flexible way to explore is by renting a car, and this is by far the most popular choice for visitors who want to see a lot of the island. Having your own car gives you the freedom to discover secluded beaches, charming mountain villages, and ancient ruins that are not easily accessible by public transport. Just remember that people here drive on the left side of the road, so if you are not used to that, it is wise to take your time at first. You will find that roads are generally well-maintained and signs are clearly marked in both Greek and English.

If you prefer not to drive, you will find that the public transport system is a budget-friendly way to travel between the major cities. A network of intercity buses connects places like Paphos, Limassol, Larnaca, and Nicosia, making it easy to travel from one urban center to another. While this can be a very convenient option for city-to-city trips, it is not ideal for reaching the more remote or rural areas, as the routes are less frequent and often do not stop at smaller attractions. For exploring within a city, local buses are also available and run on more frequent schedules.

For a slower, more active kind of exploration, cycling and walking are wonderful options. Many of the coastal cities, like Larnaca and Limassol, have beautiful promenades that are perfect for a leisurely stroll in the evening. If you enjoy hiking, the Troodos Mountains offer a vast network of nature trails with stunning scenery, and the Akamas Peninsula is a paradise for both walkers and cyclists who want to explore rugged coastal paths. While these methods are perfect for short-distance discovery and getting to know a specific area intimately, they are not practical for covering long distances across the island.

Health and Safety

When you travel to South Cyprus, you can feel confident knowing that it is a very safe and healthy destination. Still, being prepared with some essential information can give you complete peace of mind. The most important number to remember is **112**. This is the universal emergency contact for police, fire, or ambulance services across the island and all of Europe. You will be able to speak with an English-speaking operator who can direct the help you need to your exact location. Having this number saved in your phone is a small but crucial step to ensuring you are ready for any situation.

Even though you hope to never use it, having good **travel insurance** is a very wise choice before you leave home. This gives you a safety net for any unexpected medical emergencies, and it can also cover other things like cancelled flights or lost luggage. It is important to make sure your policy provides comprehensive coverage and that you read the fine print to understand exactly what you are protected against. For those of you who are citizens of the European Union, your European Health Insurance Card is also a valuable resource, but remember that it is not a full substitute for comprehensive travel insurance, as it may not cover all of your expenses.

Should you ever need medical attention, you will find that the medical facilities in South Cyprus are of a very high standard. The main cities all have modern hospitals and private clinics, where the care is excellent. For minor ailments, it is very easy to find a pharmacy. They are plentiful and often marked with a green cross. Pharmacists here are very knowledgeable and can offer you advice and over-the-counter remedies for a range of issues, from sunburn to a simple cold. Being prepared with these few details means you can relax and enjoy your trip knowing you are in good hands.

CITIES & REGIONS OVERVIEW

Nicosia: The Divided Capital

Nicosia, known as the last divided capital in Europe, has a history deeply marked by conflict and separation. The city has been the capital of Cyprus since the 10th century and boasts over 5,500 years of continuous habitation. Yet, despite its rich past, Nicosia today remains split into two parts—one controlled by Greek Cypriots in the south, and the other by Turkish Cypriots in the north, separated by a buffer zone maintained by the United Nations.

The division dates back to the early 1960s after Cyprus gained independence from British rule in 1960. Tensions between the Greek and Turkish communities escalated quickly, leading to violent clashes in 1963. By 1964, these tensions had become so severe that the city was physically divided into Greek and Turkish quarters. This division was further strengthened after Turkey's military invasion of Cyprus in 1974, which led to the establishment of the Turkish-controlled northern part of the island, including northern Nicosia. Since then, the city has lived with a palpable line of separation, often called the "Green Line," representing not just a physical boundary but also the division in culture, administration, and daily life.

Walking through Nicosia, you can see this contrast clearly. The southern part feels like a vibrant, modern European city where Greek culture thrives alongside the government and financial centers. On the northern side, you will notice a distinct Turkish influence, visible in the architecture, street names, and cultural landmarks. Efforts to unify or at least ease the division have been ongoing, especially since Cyprus joined the European Union, but the city remains a living symbol of the broader political struggles on the island.

Visiting Nicosia, you'll experience its unique atmosphere shaped by this division—a city with two identities yet one history. The dual nature of Nicosia offers a deep insight into the complexities of Cyprus itself, inviting you to explore both sides to understand its full story. This city isn't just a place to visit; it's a powerful reminder of resilience and the hope for reconciliation.

Limassol: History Meets Modernity

Limassol is a city where history and modern life come together in a fascinating way. Positioned on the southern coast of Cyprus, it is the island's second-largest city and a bustling port. Limassol's roots stretch back to ancient times, situated between the ancient city-kingdoms of Amathus and Kourion, with human activity in the area dating as far back as the Neolithic period.

Its significant historical moment came in 1191 when Richard the Lionheart landed here during the Third Crusade. Richard captured the island from the Byzantine governor and later married Berengaria of Navarre in Limassol, marking the end of Byzantine rule and the beginning of Lusignan rule. This initiated a prosperous period for the city that lasted for centuries as it became a vital center for trade and culture.

Later, the Venetians and then the Ottomans ruled Limassol, bringing different influences but also challenges. The Ottomans captured the city in the 16th century, which affected Limassol's development negatively for a time under their control.

Limassol's modern resurgence began in the late 19th century under British administration, gradually transforming into a dynamic city. Today, you will find a city that is both cosmopolitan and vibrant, with a rich blend of its historical legacy and contemporary lifestyle. It boasts luxury hotels, lively festivals, and a thriving port while preserving remnants of its medieval past, including castles and historic neighborhoods.

Visiting Limassol, you get to experience a place where the past truly meets the present, offering a deep sense of its heritage alongside all the comforts and excitement of modern urban life. This contrast makes Limassol a unique destination to explore and enjoy.

Larnaca: Coastal Charm and Culture

Larnaca is a charming coastal city that beautifully blends history, culture, and a relaxed seaside vibe. When you visit, you'll find it instantly welcoming with its warm Mediterranean atmosphere and a coastline lined with sandy beaches and a lively promenade that's perfect for strolls and people-watching.

What truly makes Larnaca special is its rich history evident everywhere you look. One of its most famous landmarks is the Church of Saint Lazarus, which dates back over a thousand years. Built on the tomb of Lazarus—who, according to tradition, was raised from the dead by Jesus and later became Larnaca's first bishop—this church is a remarkable mix of early Christian and Gothic architecture. Inside, you can feel the deep religious significance and see beautiful icons and artwork that have been preserved through centuries.

Not far from the promenade stands Larnaca Castle, a fortress originally built in the 14th century to protect the city from invaders. Over the years, it has seen rule by various powers, including the Byzantines, Venetians, Ottomans, and the British. Today, the castle houses a museum where you can discover artifacts that tell stories of the island's turbulent past, from old weapons to pottery and coins. Climbing the castle walls offers a stunning view of the sea and the city, making it a memorable spot for history lovers and photographers alike.

For a dive into Ottoman history, you can explore the beautifully preserved Ottoman baths, an architectural gem with intricate tile work that offers a glimpse into the traditional bathing culture of the time. Nearby, the Turkish Quarter (Skala) brings the old city to life with its narrow streets, artisan workshops, and charming cafes where you can enjoy local treats like loukoumades.

Beyond its historical layers, Larnaca lives and breathes modern life, with Europe Square showcasing British colonial architecture and vibrant cultural events. Here, you'll find museums, galleries, and outdoor cafes buzzing with both locals and visitors. Whether you're relaxing by the beach, exploring ancient Kition's archaeological ruins, or soaking in the diverse cultural influences, Larnaca invites you to experience a perfect mix of coastal charm and deep-rooted heritage. It's a place where history isn't just in the past—it's part of the everyday rhythm of the city.

Paphos: Ancient Ruins and Seaside Beauty

Paphos is a captivating city where ancient ruins and seaside beauty come together to create a truly special experience. As you explore Paphos, you step into a rich tapestry of history that spans thousands of years, visible all around you in the well-preserved archaeological sites and mosaics that make this city a UNESCO World Heritage Site.

The heart of Paphos lies in the Kato Paphos Archaeological Park, a vast open-air museum where you can walk among the remains of an ancient Greek and Roman city. Here, you discover four magnificent Roman villas—each famous for its stunning mosaic floors that tell stories from Greek mythology. The House of Dionysos, the House of Orpheus, the House of Theseus, and the House of Aion stand out with their intricate designs that have survived for centuries, inviting you to imagine life in the Roman era.

As you wander through the park, you'll also encounter key structures like an ancient agora (marketplace), a theatre used for performances centuries ago, the Asklepieion temple dedicated to the god of medicine, and early Christian basilicas that reveal the city's shift through different cultural phases over time.

Just nearby, the Tombs of the Kings offer a striking contrast—these rock-cut tombs, carved out of solid stone, served as burial sites for nobles and high-ranking officials rather than actual kings. Their grand designs and impressive size speak to the importance of those laid to rest there. Walking through these tombs, you get a sense of reverence and mystery that deepens your connection to the past.

Beyond the ruins, Paphos itself is a seaside town with a relaxed, scenic charm. The coastline, dotted with beaches and a charming harbor, offers beautiful views and a chance to unwind after exploring the ancient sites. Here, history meets the present in a seamless blend, allowing you to enjoy the sun, sea, and rich cultural heritage all in one place.

Being in Paphos means immersing yourself in a living history lesson while soaking up the beauty of Cyprus's southwestern shore—a place where every stone and wave tells a story of the island's fascinating past and vibrant present.

Troodos Mountains: Nature and Adventure

The Troodos Mountains are the largest mountain range in Cyprus, covering about a third of the island, mainly on the western and southern parts. At the heart of these mountains is Mount Olympus, the highest peak, rising to 1,952 meters (6,404 feet). The range features steep valleys and rugged igneous rock formations, surrounded by dense forests of pine, cedar, cypress, and oak. The peaks are often snow-covered during winter months, creating a distinct mountain climate different from the coastal regions.

When you visit the Troodos Mountains, you experience a natural playground rich in outdoor activities. The area is famous for hiking, with many marked trails offering scenic views, waterfalls, and encounters with local wildlife. The villages scattered throughout the mountains are charming and offer a glimpse of traditional Cypriot life, with stone houses, narrow streets, and friendly locals.

The mountains are also steeped in history and culture. You can visit several Byzantine monasteries and churches scattered among the peaks, known for their beautiful frescoes and historical significance. The Troodos area was an important mining center in antiquity, especially for copper, which played a crucial role in Cyprus's development throughout history.

Summers in Troodos offer a refreshing escape from the heat of the coast, with cooler temperatures and fresh mountain air. Winters bring a quieter, snowy landscape that invites winter sports and cozy mountain hospitality.

Exploring Troodos means immersing yourself in nature, adventure, and history all at once, making it a must-visit region if you're looking to experience the green heart of Cyprus and enjoy a peaceful yet exciting mountain retreat.

Ayia Napa And Protaras: Sun, Sand, and Nightlife

Ayia Napa and Protaras are two of Cyprus's most popular destinations when you're looking for a mix of sun, sand, and nightlife, but each offers a different vibe suited to different tastes.

Ayia Napa is famously known as the nightlife capital of Cyprus. If you like the idea of beach days filled with sunbathing and water activities, followed by lively nights, this is the place for you. Nissi Beach, one of the island's most popular, is the hotspot for day parties and music from top DJs. When the sun sets, the town comes alive with countless nightclubs, bars, and discos where you can dance until the early hours. If you want a buzzing atmosphere with plenty of entertainment options, Ayia Napa does not disappoint. Besides parties, there are also more chilled-out spots like the Hard Rock Café or unique experiences such as the Underwater Sculpture Museum to explore during quieter moments.

Protaras, just a short drive from Ayia Napa, offers a different pace. It's quieter and more laid-back, making it ideal if you want to enjoy crystal-clear waters and sandy beaches without the intense party scene. Fig Tree Bay is the crown jewel of Protaras, known for its gorgeous clean beach and calm atmosphere perfect for relaxing or romantic walks. While Protaras doesn't have as wild a nightlife, it still offers a good selection of bars and pubs, including lounges and karaoke clubs, where you can enjoy an easygoing evening. This makes it a great choice if you want a balance between some nightlife and peaceful beach time.

If you are staying in Protaras but want a night out, Ayia Napa is just a 15-minute drive away, so you can enjoy the best of both worlds without missing out. From buzzing beach parties to quiet seaside dinners, this area gives you plenty of options. Whether you're into lively clubbing or serene coastline walks, Ayia Napa and Protaras together are a perfect combo for a varied and fun holiday on the southeast coast of Cyprus.

MUST-SEE ATTRACTIONS

Nicosia

Ledra Street and the Green Line

Ledra Street is one of the most famous and symbolic streets in Nicosia, the divided capital of Cyprus. This bustling pedestrian thoroughfare runs through the heart of the city, linking the Greek Cypriot south to the Turkish Cypriot north. Historically, Ledra Street was a vibrant commercial center and the main shopping street of Nicosia. However, its significance goes far beyond shopping—it stands as a powerful emblem of division and hope for reunification in Cyprus.

The Green Line, also known as the United Nations Buffer Zone, cuts through the northern end of Ledra Street, dividing the city between the two communities. For decades, this line represented a hard border, sealed off and guarded, a physical reminder of the tensions and conflicts that arose in the 1960s and escalated after the Turkish invasion in 1974. The barricade on Ledra Street stood as a stark symbol of the division and was often referred to as a "murder mile" during earlier conflicts due to its violent history.

In April 2008, after over 30 years, the roadblock on Ledra Street was reopened to pedestrians, allowing people to cross between the north and south parts of Nicosia. This crossing has since become one of the most visited and photographed spots in the city, where visitors can physically experience the division while witnessing efforts toward greater interaction and peace. Walking through the street, you'll encounter a lively atmosphere filled with shops, cafes, and street vendors on the southern side, while the northern part presents a glimpse into Turkish Cypriot culture and architecture.

On the southern end, you can explore areas near Eleftheria Square and see notable spots such as the Shacolas Tower, which offers panoramic views of Nicosia and the Green Line. The street itself is an interesting mix of the old and the new, with restored buildings alongside some that still show the marks of past conflicts. The experience of crossing the Green Line here is unique because you get a direct sense of the historical and ongoing complexities of Cyprus.

For practical details, Ledra Street is open and accessible to visitors every day during daylight hours, generally from morning until early evening, but the exact times can vary depending on political circumstances and local regulations. There is no entrance fee to walk along Ledra Street or to cross the Green Line checkpoint on foot, though crossing requires passing through a controlled checkpoint where identification is checked. The crossing is pedestrian-only, connecting two parts of Nicosia through the buffer zone under United Nations monitoring. Ledra Street is located right at the city center, starting at Eleftheria Square in the south and ending at the UN buffer zone near the northern entrance.

Visiting Ledra Street and crossing the Green Line is a compelling experience, offering both a powerful lesson in history and a hopeful glimpse into Cyprus's future as a place where two communities live side by side. It is a must-see attraction in Nicosia for anyone wanting to understand the city's unique character and the island's complex past and present.

The Selimiye Mosque (Cathedral of Saint Sophia)

The Selimiye Mosque, originally known as the Cathedral of Saint Sophia, stands as one of North Nicosia's most impressive and historically rich landmarks. This striking building uniquely combines French Gothic architecture with Ottoman mosque features, showcasing a layered history that reaches back to the 13th century. Originally constructed as a Roman Catholic cathedral, its building began in 1209 and was completed in 1326. Its design reflects the influence of the Lusignan kings who ruled Cyprus during the Crusades, intending it to be a grand symbol of their reign and faith. The stonework, soaring vaulted ceilings, and the ornate façade evoke a medieval European cathedral, while the two minarets and Islamic interior elements speak to its later transformation.

When the Ottomans captured Nicosia in 1570, the cathedral was converted into a mosque, marking a significant cultural shift. The Islamic features, including a mihrab, minbar, whitewashed walls, and reoriented layout toward Mecca, were added, blending respectfully with the original Gothic structure. Despite these changes, the building retains much of its medieval charm, with four marble columns from Ancient Salamis placed in the apse and the distinctive west front showcasing three differently styled decorated doorways. It serves not only as a place of worship but also as a symbol of Nicosia's complex history and multicultural heritage.

When you visit Selimiye Mosque, you can explore this architectural masterpiece that comfortably accommodates around 2,500 worshippers and offers a unique insight into Cyprus's religious and political past. To catch the mosque in its most tranquil and atmospheric moments, plan your visit just before or after one of the five daily prayer sessions, as non-Muslims are asked to avoid visiting during prayer times. You will notice the blend of cultural influences as you walk through its vast interior, experiencing an incredible fusion of Gothic elegance and Ottoman spiritual design.

The mosque is open daily from sunrise to sunset, welcoming visitors without an entrance fee. However, modest dress is required as a sign of respect, so you should wear long skirts or trousers and shirts that cover your shoulders. Women are also asked to cover their heads with a scarf, which you can borrow at the entrance if needed. Situated in the heart of North Nicosia, near other significant historical sites, the Selimiye Mosque is easy to access and forms an essential part of any visit to the city.

Visiting the Selimiye Mosque is more than just a sightseeing trip—it's an immersive experience that connects you to centuries of history, faith, and culture intertwined in one of Cyprus's most iconic buildings. Whether you are drawn by its architecture, its history, or its spiritual ambiance, this landmark leaves a lasting impression of the island's layered identity and the ongoing story of coexistence and change.

The Cyprus Museum

The Cyprus Museum in Nicosia stands as the island's oldest and largest archaeological museum, making it an essential destination for anyone interested in uncovering the rich history of Cyprus. Established in 1882 during British rule, this museum was founded to protect and preserve the island's unparalleled archaeological heritage, especially after concerns about antiquities being taken off the island. Located in the heart of Nicosia on Museum Street, the building itself holds historical significance, constructed between 1908 and 1924 with subsequent expansions to accommodate its growing collection.

When you visit the Cyprus Museum, you embark on a captivating journey through the island's past, tracing human activity from the Neolithic era, around 10,000 BC, through to the Early Byzantine period in the 7th century AD. The museum's exhibits are arranged in chronological and thematic order, allowing you to follow the development of Cypriot civilization over thousands of years. You will encounter an extensive variety of artifacts such as pottery, intricate jewellery, stone sculptures, coins, tools made of copper, and remarkable tomb offerings. Among the highlights is the famous statue of Aphrodite of Soloi, as well as stunning Bronze Age treasures including golden jewellery and finely crafted pottery. The museum also features impressive Roman mosaics that depict scenes from mythology and everyday life, offering a vivid glimpse into the cultural influences that shaped Cyprus.

The Cyprus Museum is more than just a collection of old objects; it presents Cyprus as a crossroads of civilizations, reflecting influences from ancient Greeks, Romans, Byzantines, and earlier settlers. Its archaeological displays also tell stories about religious practices, trade, burial customs, and everyday life through the ages, making it a rich and informative experience for visitors.

To make the most of your visit, plan enough time to explore all fourteen display halls that surround a central courtyard where additional museum facilities are located, including a library and conservation labs. The museum is wheelchair accessible, with ramps, chair lifts, and disabled toilets to assist all visitors.

The museum is open throughout the year, with operating hours generally from Tuesday to Friday 8:00 AM to 6:00 PM, Saturday 9:00 AM to 5:00 PM, and Sunday 10:00 AM to 1:00 PM. It is closed on Mondays, Christmas Day, New Year's Day, and Easter Sunday following the Greek Orthodox calendar. Notably, every first Wednesday of the month, the museum remains open until 8:00 PM for longer visits. Entrance to the Cyprus Museum is free, making it an accessible cultural gem for all visitors. Its central location in Nicosia means it is easy to reach, nestled near other historical sites and city landmarks.

Walking down the Cyprus Museum offers a deep, immersive experience into the island's vast archaeological history — it is truly a treasure for history enthusiasts, families, and curious travelers wanting to connect intimately with the ancient civilizations that shaped Cyprus. This is a must-see attraction that will leave you with a greater appreciation for the island's past and its rich cultural legacy.

Famagusta Gate

Famagusta Gate is one of Nicosia's most striking historical landmarks, serving as a grand entrance through the city's famous Venetian walls. Built in 1567 by the Venetians, it was initially called Porta Giuliana in honor of Giulio Savorgnano, the engineer responsible for designing the impressive fortified walls encircling the old city. This gate was not just a functional entryway but a masterpiece of Renaissance military architecture. Its design was inspired by the Lazaretto Gate of Candia (modern Heraklion, Crete), featuring a massive vaulted passage topped by an eleven-meter-wide dome with a circular opening, reminiscent of Rome's Pantheon.

Famagusta Gate originally opened onto the road leading to the important port town of Famagusta, which is how it got its modern name. The structure has been carefully preserved over centuries, including a significant restoration carried out by the Ottomans in 1821. During Ottoman rule, it saw practical adjustments such as the addition of a lookout and strict regulations on who could pass through—only Turks were allowed to ride horses through the gate, while Christians and foreigners had to proceed on foot. It was also locked during the night and on Fridays for prayer, emphasizing its role in the social order of the time.

Visiting Famagusta Gate today offers you more than just a walk through a historical doorway. The interior has been repurposed into a vibrant cultural center where exhibitions, concerts, and theater performances breathe new life into this ancient gate. You can admire the meticulous stonework of the great archway and the impressive dome overhead, imagining how this gate once stood strong as a vital defense point guarding the city from invasion. Be sure to explore the surrounding area, Taht-el-Kale, a regenerated neighborhood full of charming cafes, shops, and other cultural spots that help paint the picture of Nicosia's rich, layered past.

For practical information, Famagusta Gate is located on the eastern side of Nicosia's Venetian walls, making it a central and accessible landmark within the old town. The gate and the cultural space inside are open to visitors typically during standard daytime hours, though the exact opening times can vary and it's best to check in advance to confirm the schedule, especially since it occasionally closes for restoration works or special events. Entry to the cultural center is usually free, inviting you to enjoy the art and performances hosted within this historical setting. When you visit, it's a good idea to allow enough time to fully appreciate both the architectural beauty and the cultural events that highlight the continued importance of this gate in Nicosia's vibrant city life.

Famagusta Gate stands as a powerful symbol of Nicosia's past resilience and present creativity, making it a must-see destination for anyone wanting to connect with the city's Venetian heritage and explore one of the most fascinating gateways through time in Cyprus. It offers a unique blend of history, art, and culture all within a magnificent architectural frame, ensuring your visit will be both enriching and memorable.

The Venetian Walls and Bastions

The Venetian Walls and Bastions of Nicosia stand as one of the most remarkable historical features of the city, marking its rich and turbulent past. Built between 1567 and 1570 during Venetian rule, these walls were designed to defend the city against the looming threat of the Ottoman Empire. The decision to build these fortifications came after the Great Siege of Malta, when the Venetians realized the importance of strong defenses in the Mediterranean. The walls replaced earlier medieval fortifications, which were considered inadequate for the evolving nature of warfare in the Renaissance period.

The walls of Nicosia form a nearly circular shape with a circumference of about five kilometers (approximately three miles). They enclose the historic old city and are punctuated by eleven pentagonal bastions with rounded orillons (protective projections). These bastions were named after prominent Venetian officials and Cypriot aristocrats of the time, who contributed funds to their construction. Each bastion, such as the Caraffa, Podocattaro, and D'Avila Bastions, carries its own story of bravery, loyalty, and tragedy connected to the defense of the city during the Ottoman siege in 1570.

In addition to the bastions, the walls are fortified with three main gates: the Famagusta Gate, Paphos Gate, and Kyrenia Gate. These gates were essential for controlling access to the city and are still notable architectural landmarks today. The design of the walls and bastions reflects the advanced military thinking of the Renaissance, incorporating principles that allowed for better deflection of cannon fire and improved defensive capabilities, even though the walls were still incomplete when the Ottomans eventually captured the city.

As you walk along these walls, you will notice the thick stone fortifications and the strategic layout that once made Nicosia a stronghold against invasion. The bastions provide elevated vantage points offering panoramic views of the city and its surroundings, making them a favorite spot for visitors to pause and soak in the historic atmosphere. The moat surrounding the walls, once filled with water as part of the defensive system, has now been transformed into a scenic park area inviting leisurely strolls.

The walls stand not just as a physical barrier of the past but as a symbol of Nicosia's resilience and the enduring legacy of its diverse history. This impressive fortification encapsulates the city's role as a crossroads of cultures and conflicts in the Eastern Mediterranean.

The Venetian Walls and Bastions are located in the heart of Nicosia, encircling the old city. They are accessible to the public every day, with no entrance fee to explore the exterior walls and walk along the bastions. While the walls themselves do not have formal opening or closing times, some of the gates and cultural sites within the walls, such as Famagusta Gate cultural center, have specific hours and occasional closures for events or restoration.

Touring the Venetian Walls and Bastions gives you an immersive experience into Renaissance military architecture and Nicosia's layered history. You can explore the bastions and gates at your own pace and enjoy the contrast of this ancient defense system with the bustling modern city just beyond its borders, making it a must-see attraction when in Nicosia.

Limassol

The Kourion Archaeological Site

The Kourion Archaeological Site near Limassol is an extraordinary window into the ancient past of Cyprus, offering a journey through time from Neolithic origins to the Roman and Byzantine eras. This impressive site, perched on a hill overlooking the fertile valley of the Kouris River, was once a powerful city-kingdom believed to have been founded by settlers from Argos in the Late Bronze Age. Over thousands of years, Kourion evolved into a bustling center for trade, culture, and governance. Although it faced destruction from a massive earthquake in 365 AD and later Arab raids in the 7th century, much of its history is still beautifully preserved for visitors like you to explore.

When you walk through Kourion, the highlight is unquestionably the ancient theatre, a stunning architectural marvel that could seat up to 3,500 spectators. Dating back to the 2nd or 3rd century AD, this theatre remains remarkably intact and even hosts cultural performances today, allowing you to connect with the vibrant life that once animated this city. Beyond the theatre, you will come across the remains of a 3rd-century Roman agora (marketplace), a public bath complex, and a Nymphaeum, which together reveal the daily and social life of an advanced Roman city.

Another must-see is the House of Achilles, a 4th-century reception center adorned with exquisite mosaic floors that depict mythological scenes. Equally impressive is the House of the Gladiators, named for its mosaics showing gladiatorial combats, transporting you to moments of ancient entertainment. The complex of Eustolios offers insights into early Christian life, showcasing a private residence with bath facilities from the 4th to 5th century AD. Adding to this is an early Christian basilica from the same period, highlighting the religious evolution within Kourion.

While the main archaeological park contains these treasures, you can also explore nearby sites a bit further out, such as the remains of an ancient stadium and the Sanctuary of Apollo Hylates, a revered religious center. A small visitors' center at the site helps orient you and offers a scale model of the area for better understanding before you begin your exploration.

Kourion is located about 19 kilometers west of Limassol, and the easiest way to reach it is by car or taxi. The site is generally open to visitors every day, with hours often from early morning until late afternoon or early evening, but it's advisable to check exact times as they can change seasonally. Entrance fees are modest and provide access to one of Cyprus's richest archaeological experiences. Photography is allowed, and comfortable walking shoes are recommended, as the site covers a large area with uneven terrain.

The Kourion Archaeological Site offers you a fascinating combination of scenic views, remarkable ancient architecture, and a vivid story of an influential city that shaped Cyprus through millennia. It's a perfect destination if you want to dive deep into history while enjoying the beautiful coastal landscape near Limassol.

The Amathus Ruins

The Amathus Ruins offer a fascinating glimpse into one of the oldest and most significant ancient city-kingdoms of Cyprus, situated about 10 kilometers east of Limassol on a scenic hill overlooking the coast. This archaeological site holds layers of history spanning more than 3,000 years, with origins that are believed to date back to around 1100 BC when Greek island settlers first established the city. According to local mythology, Amathus is famously linked to the story of Ariadne, who was left here after her escape with Theseus and later died during childbirth.

As you explore Amathus, you will discover the remains of an ancient agora, or marketplace, which is still well-preserved, including its paved stone floor and the faint outlines of public fountains. Near the agora, you can make out the foundations of an elaborate aqueduct system that once supplied fresh water to the city. Scattered around the site are ruins of houses from the Hellenistic period, defensive walls partially preserved that guarded the city, and the ruins of a 5th-century Early Christian basilica near the base of the hill.

Climbing higher to the acropolis, you come across the ruins of temples dedicated to Aphrodite and Hercules, hinting at the religious and cultural life that once flourished here. From this vantage point on the hillside, enjoy sweeping views of the city below and the Mediterranean Sea beyond.

Amathus thrived through various historical phases, ruled at different times by Greeks, Phoenicians, Persians, Ptolemies, and Romans, which is evident in the architectural remains and artifacts found here. Despite its prosperity, the city was abandoned around the 7th century AD, likely due to Arab invasions, and remained forgotten until rediscovered by British archaeologists in the 19th century.

For visitors, the site opens a window to ancient urban life, commerce, faith, and city defense strategies spread over a large area, making it ideal for a day-long exploration. The site is open year-round, with differing seasonal hours that generally start in the early morning and close by early evening. Admission is modest, making it accessible without burdening your travel budget.

When planning your visit, it's recommended to wear comfortable walking shoes and to bring water and sun protection, especially in the hotter months, since the archaeological site is expansive and largely exposed to the sun. The ruins are easily reachable by car or taxi from Limassol, which is just a short drive away along the coastal road.

Limassol Castle and Medieval Museum

Limassol Castle is a formidable medieval fortress that sits proudly near the old harbor in the heart of Limassol's historic center. As you approach this castle, you instantly recognize its striking presence, a stone structure heavily shaped by centuries of history. The origins of the castle are believed to date back to the Byzantine era, around the 4th to 7th century AD, built over the ruins of an Early Christian basilica and later a Middle Byzantine monument. According to tradition, Guy de Lusignan, who founded the Lusignan dynasty in Cyprus, constructed the original fortification around 1193. This castle has witnessed numerous defining moments throughout the island's history, including its connection to the legendary King Richard the Lionheart, who is said to have married Berengaria of Navarre within its walls in 1191.

The castle you see today mainly reflects the architectural style from the period of Ottoman rule, around 1590, following a series of reconstructions and fortifications. Over the centuries, the castle endured attacks from Genoese, Mameluks, and earthquakes, leading to repeated cycles of damage and repair. Its robust stone walls, arched gateways, and strong towers tell the story of its defensive role, protecting the strategic harbor and the city from invasions. You can still see details that showcase a blend of Byzantine, Lusignan, Venetian, and Ottoman influences, including Gothic arches from the Lusignan period along with Ottoman additions.

Inside, Limassol Castle serves as home to the Cyprus Medieval Museum. Walking through its rooms, you will find fascinating exhibits featuring medieval artifacts such as armor, weaponry, coins, pottery, religious items, and everyday objects from the island's medieval era. This museum offers an immersive glimpse into the lives of the castle's former inhabitants and the broader social, economic, and artistic development of Cyprus from the 3rd to the 18th century. The castle's interior also houses parts of the old prison cells that were in use until 1950, adding to the historical atmosphere as you explore the grounds.

Climbing the castle towers offers magnificent views of Limassol city and the sparkling Mediterranean Sea, a reminder of the castle's strategic importance and its role shaping the coastal city. The courtyard often hosts cultural events, including concerts and exhibitions, creating a lively space that bridges the past with the present.

When planning your visit, you will find Limassol Castle conveniently located near the old harbor, making it easy to access in the historic center of Limassol. The castle and the Medieval Museum are open to visitors most days, generally from morning until late afternoon, but it's best to check exact opening hours ahead of time as they may vary seasonally. Admission typically involves a modest fee, around 4.50 euros, making it an affordable and enriching cultural stop on your itinerary. Note that the castle's site is not wheelchair accessible due to its medieval structure and uneven surfaces.

The castle embodies Limassol's rich heritage, blending architectural beauty, historical significance, and engaging museum exhibits to offer a truly memorable experience of Cyprus's medieval past. Whether you are a history lover, cultural explorer, or simply curious traveler, this landmark is a must-see highlight when exploring Limassol.

Fasouri Watermania Waterpark

Fasouri Watermania Waterpark is the largest waterpark in Cyprus, located in Fasouri Village, about a 15-minute drive from the center of Limassol. Spanning approximately 25 acres, this waterpark offers a tropical Polynesian-themed setting that blends natural green spaces with thrilling water attractions. Since opening in 1999, the park has expanded several times and now welcomes thousands of visitors each year, making it a top destination for families, friends, and tourists looking for fun and relaxation in the sun.

At Fasouri Watermania, you'll find over 30 different water slides and attractions suitable for all ages and thrill levels. Among the highlights are one of the largest wave pools in Europe, a lazy river inviting you to float along gently, and several high-adrenaline slides like the Black Hole and Kamikaze slides. The waterpark is designed to entertain everyone—from young children enjoying the dedicated kids' activity pools and splash areas to adults seeking exciting rides and a lively atmosphere. Beyond the slides, the park provides ample sunbeds—over 2,000 for you to lounge on—along with plenty of shaded areas to relax between rides.

There are three restaurants and several snack bars scattered across the park, serving a variety of tasty dishes and refreshments that keep you fueled throughout your visit. The facilities include locker rentals to keep your belongings safe, a souvenir shop with beachwear and accessories, and additional services like a fish spa and massage parlor for moments of indulgence. Lifeguards and staff are numerous and well-trained, ensuring your safety and comfort during your day at the park.

For practical information, Fasouri Watermania is open seasonally, generally from 10:00 AM to 6:00 PM on days it operates, with closures typically on Mondays and Tuesdays or outside the high season, so it's good to check in advance. The entrance fee as of 2025 is around 33 to 36 euros per adult, with discounts available for children and families. Access to the waterpark includes free parking in a large lot with about 750 spaces. The park is wheelchair accessible, making it welcoming to guests with varying needs. Note that children under 12 must be accompanied by an adult, and swimming attire guidelines are strictly enforced for safety reasons.

Located just off the Limassol-Paphos highway, Fasouri Watermania is easy to reach by car or taxi. This destination promises a full day of excitement, blending natural beauty, fun water experiences, and excellent service to create a memorable outing suited to visitors of all ages. Whether you're looking to cool off, challenge yourself on daring slides, or relax in a vibrant yet safe environment, Fasouri Watermania Waterpark stands out as a must-visit attraction near Limassol that delivers both thrills and tropical charm.

Kolossi Castle

Kolossi Castle, located just 14 kilometers west of Limassol near the village of Kolossi, is a well-preserved medieval fortress that offers a rich journey into Cyprus's Crusader past. Originally built around 1210 by the Knights Hospitallers, a Catholic military order charged with protecting Crusader territories, this castle held strategic importance due to its fortified position and its role in the production of sugar from the surrounding sugarcane plantations—one of Cyprus's main exports in the Middle Ages. The castle you see today was reconstructed in 1454 under the order of Louis de Magnac, whose coat of arms still adorns the walls, following destruction caused by raids in the earlier 15th century.

When you visit Kolossi Castle, you will enter a three-story square keep surrounded by a large rectangular enclosure. The castle's thick stone walls, narrow windows for defense, and crenellations reflect its original military purpose, designed to withstand attacks and protect its valuable assets. Climbing from the basement up to the roof, you can take in sweeping views of the surrounding countryside, imagining the castle's former role as an important command center and watchtower. Nearby, you'll find the ruins of a 14th-century sugar mill, highlighting the castle's historic connection to sugar production, a significant industry at the time.

Besides its military and economic importance, Kolossi is also famous for being associated with Commandaria, one of the oldest named wines in the world. Legend has it that after King Richard the Lionheart married Berengaria of Navarre at nearby Limassol, he declared this sweet Cypriot wine to be "the wine of kings and the king of wines." This local sweet wine continues to be a symbol of the region's heritage and is a delightful complement to your visit.

Kolossi Castle is open throughout the year, with visiting hours typically from early morning to late afternoon or early evening, varying with the seasons. From mid-April to mid-September, it is generally open from around 8:30 AM until 7:30 PM, while between mid-September and mid-April, the hours are roughly 8:30 AM to 5:00 PM. The entrance fee is quite affordable, about 2.50 euros, inviting you to explore without a heavy cost. The castle is easily accessible by car with on-site parking available, and there is also a bus stop nearby (Bus Number 17) within walking distance for those using public transport.

This historic site not only provides insight into the island's military and economic past but also offers a peaceful, scenic setting that connects you to centuries of Cyprus's heritage. Whether you are a history enthusiast or simply enjoy exploring magnificent old castles, Kolossi is a rewarding destination to include in your Limassol itinerary.

Larnaca

Larnaca Salt Lake and Hala Sultan Tekke

Larnaca Salt Lake and Hala Sultan Tekke are two of the most captivating attractions you'll want to experience when visiting Larnaca, offering a perfect blend of natural beauty and cultural significance.

Larnaca Salt Lake is a striking natural landmark just a few kilometers from the city center. Covering around six square kilometers, the lake transforms dramatically throughout the year, sometimes shimmering with crystal-clear water and at other times drying out to reveal salt flats. The most enchanting time to visit is during the winter months when the lake becomes a sanctuary for thousands of migratory flamingos and other bird species. Watching these elegant birds wading in the shallow waters or flying gracefully against the vivid sky is a breathtaking sight, making it a favorite spot for nature lovers and photographers. Beyond the flamingos, the lake's tranquil atmosphere invites you to enjoy peaceful walks along its perimeter, where you can soak in the calmness and observe diverse plant life adapted to the salty environment.

Close to the lake lies Hala Sultan Tekke, a beautiful mosque complex set beside its banks. This sacred site is one of the most important Islamic landmarks in Cyprus and draws visitors seeking a quiet, reflective experience. You will be greeted by serene courtyards, iconic minarets, and stunning Ottoman architecture framed by palm trees and the lake beyond. The peaceful setting creates a harmonious blend of history and nature that's inviting whether you are interested in spirituality, culture, or simply looking for a tranquil place to unwind. Visitors are welcome to explore the grounds respectfully, and you can appreciate the mosque's intricate details and the ambiance that makes it a unique place on the island.

Practical details to plan your visit: The Larnaca Salt Lake and Hala Sultan Tekke are easily reachable by car or taxi from the city center in about 10 minutes, and there are parking facilities nearby. The Salt Lake is an open natural site, so there is no entrance fee or timed opening hours—you can visit during daylight to enjoy the best views and birdwatching opportunities. Hala Sultan Tekke is generally open daily from early morning until late afternoon, but it's best to avoid visiting during prayer times for a respectful experience. Entrance to the mosque is free, though modest dress is required, and visitors should be mindful of the peaceful surroundings.

Whether you come for the flamingos, the sunset reflections on the salt flats, or the quiet beauty of the mosque, you'll leave with a sense of calm and wonder.

Larnaca Castle

Larnaca Castle, also known as Larnaca Medieval Castle or Larnaca Fort, is a captivating historic landmark located at the southern end of the Finikoudes promenade, right by the Mediterranean Sea. This fortress, dating back to the late 12th century and expanded significantly during the reign of King James I between 1382 and 1398, was originally built to defend the southern coast of Cyprus and protect the important harbor of Larnaca. Over the centuries, the castle has witnessed a fascinating evolution, serving various roles including a military fortification, an artillery station, a prison during the British colonial period, and now a museum.

When you visit Larnaca Castle, you can immerse yourself in centuries of history as you explore its stone walls, red-tiled roofs, and scenic surroundings enhanced by palm trees and lush floral displays. The castle's strategic position overlooking the sea offers breathtaking views, making it an ideal place not only to learn about Cyprus's layered history but also to enjoy the calming coastal atmosphere. Stepping inside, you'll find a collection of rooms housing a small museum that exhibits artifacts spanning from the Early Christian period through to the Ottoman era. These relics include Muslim and Christian headstones, items related to the castle's use as a prison, including references to the execution chamber where gallows were once installed and used until 1948. The museum provides fascinating insights into the transformation of the castle and the island's complex past. During the summer months, the castle's courtyard comes alive as an open-air theater hosting plays and musical performances, with seating for around 200 guests, making your visit not just educational but also culturally enriching.

Practical details for your visit include the castle's opening hours, which vary seasonally. From mid-April to mid-September, it is generally open from 8:00 AM to 7:30 PM, and from mid-September to mid-April, the hours are approximately 8:00 AM to 5:00 PM. It welcomes visitors every day except on certain public holidays. Entrance fees are quite affordable, currently around 2.50 euros per person, with discounts available for pensioners and organized groups. The castle is situated in the heart of Larnaca, easily accessible via public transport with bus stops nearby, or by taxi or on foot from the city center. While the museum inside provides a richly detailed historical experience, the rooftop and castle grounds offer stunning panoramic views of the city skyline, Finikoudes Beach, and the shimmering Mediterranean Sea, perfect for photography and leisurely exploration.

The Zenobia Wreck Dive Site

The Zenobia Wreck Dive Site is one of the premier attractions for diving enthusiasts visiting Larnaca, Cyprus, and is widely regarded as one of the top ten wreck dives globally. The Zenobia was a Swedish-built roll-on/roll-off ferry, an impressive 172 meters long, which tragically sank on its maiden voyage on June 7, 1980. Due to a malfunction in its ballast tanks, the ship began listing and was towed out of Larnaca harbor to prevent blockage, but it eventually capsized and sank about 1.5 kilometers offshore in Larnaca Bay. The wreck now rests on its port side at a depth of approximately 42 meters, creating a sprawling underwater site that has become a magnet for divers from around the world.

Zenobia Wreck offers a thrilling dive experience with a unique blend of history and marine life. The ship's vast size and intricate interior spaces invite divers to explore multiple compartments, including the bridge, the cafeteria, and the accommodation areas, as well as cargo still aboard, notably some 135 articulated lorries chained to the ship's decks. The wreck's depth ranges from about 18 meters at the shallowest point to 42 meters at the seabed, with excellent water visibility often reaching up to 30 meters or more under good conditions. This site appeals to advanced open water divers due to its medium difficulty level and relatively low currents year-round, making it accessible to many experienced divers.

The Zenobia is not only a fascinating historical relic but also serves as an artificial reef teeming with Mediterranean marine species such as groupers, barracudas, sea bream, rainbow wrasse, ornate wrasse, damselfish, and occasionally, turtles. Its submerged structure provides a diverse habitat that enhances the dive's scenic beauty and ecological interest. Diving here often includes boat access from Larnaca, with trips commonly offering two dives on the wreck among other nearby dive sites, often complemented by amenities like BBQ lunches onshore and expert guidance from PADI-qualified dive instructors.

The Zenobia Wreck is located about 1.5 kilometers (approximately one mile) off the shore of Larnaca Bay. Access is exclusively by boat via dive centers operating out of Larnaca Marina. Dive excursions typically operate daily, weather permitting. The dive site itself is open year-round, but water temperatures vary seasonally between around 15°C and 28°C, so proper exposure protection is advised depending on the time of year. As the wreck lies at considerable depths, it is recommended for divers with at least an advanced open water certification. Equipment rental, guided tours, and safety briefings ensure a safe and enjoyable experience, and entrance fees depend on the dive operators' packages, which often include multiple dives, equipment rental, and transportation.

In summary, the Zenobia Wreck Dive Site is a must-visit for those seeking a world-class diving adventure in Cyprus. It combines an extraordinary historical underwater landmark with vibrant marine life and excellent diving conditions, creating a truly unforgettable experience under the Mediterranean waves near Larnaca.

Mackenzie Beach

Mackenzie Beach is one of the most popular and vibrant coastal destinations near Larnaca, situated just about 3 kilometers from the city center. This beach stretches for roughly 1,000 meters, with sandy shores that vary in width, sometimes reaching up to 80 meters wide, making it an inviting space whether you want to relax on the sand or enjoy the clear, calm waters of the Mediterranean. The beach benefits from a Blue Flag award, a testament to its cleanliness, safety, and high-quality facilities, making it a favored spot for families, locals, and visitors alike.

One of the unique and thrilling aspects of Mackenzie Beach is its proximity to Larnaca International Airport. Sitting almost within view of the runway, bathers and beachgoers are treated to spectacular low-flying planes arriving and departing, creating a dynamic atmosphere that's especially popular with plane-spotters and photographers. Alongside this aviation spectacle, the beach itself offers a range of activities and comfort; sunbeds and umbrellas can be rented for convenience, and lifeguards are on duty during the summer months to ensure safety for swimmers and water sports enthusiasts.

Mackenzie Beach is also known as the heart of Larnaca's nightlife and dining scene. The beachfront promenade buzzes with an array of stylish cafes, upscale restaurants, bustling bars, and vibrant nightclubs, catering to diverse tastes and moods. Whether you crave fresh seafood, international cuisine, or a tropical cocktail while enjoying a sea view, Mackenzie provides a lively culinary and social hub. During summer evenings, the area often hosts open-air concerts, beach parties, and cultural events, transforming it into a vibrant party destination.

For those who prefer a quieter day, the beach's calm and shallow waters are perfect for swimming, especially for children and less confident swimmers. The sandy bottom stretches out gently, making it safe and comfortable for a relaxed day by the sea. Sports enthusiasts can also find opportunities for water activities such as kite surfing. Additionally, children's playgrounds and outdoor exercise equipment line the beach area, catering to families and fitness lovers.

Access to Mackenzie Beach is straightforward whether traveling by car, bike, or public transport. Ample parking is available behind the row of restaurants and cafes, as well as multiple entry points with well-maintained paths leading onto the beach. For those who enjoy walking or cycling, the avenue Tassos Mitsopoulos connects the beach with Larnaca city center and other attractions, including the nearby Larnaca Salt Lake and Hala Sultan Tekke mosque, which are just a short distance away.

Facilities at Mackenzie Beach include clean toilets, showers, changing rooms, and ample seating areas to ensure a comfortable visit. Lifeguards patrol the beach generally from June through October between 10:30 AM and 6:00 PM, adding reassurance for swimmers. The beach is family-friendly during the day and becomes one of the most sought-after nightlife hotspots in Larnaca at night, striking a balance between relaxation and excitement.

Choirokoitia Neolithic Settlement

The Neolithic Settlement of Choirokoitia in Cyprus is a truly remarkable and ancient site that offers a deep dive into the earliest chapters of human civilization on the island. Dating back to around 7000 BC, this prehistoric agricultural village is among the oldest known settlements in the Eastern Mediterranean and stands as a testament to the ingenuity and communal spirit of early human societies. Nestled on the slopes of a hill near a loop of the Maroni River, about 6 kilometers from Cyprus's southern coast, Choirokoitia was home to one of the first farming communities that gradually shaped the island's cultural landscape.

Visitors to Choirokoitia are greeted by well-preserved archaeological remains alongside expertly reconstructed circular dwellings characteristic of Neolithic architecture. These homes were made from mudbrick and stone, featuring flat roofs and arranged in clusters around small courtyards where domestic and social activities thrived. The settlement was fortified with protective walls, indicating the collective effort and advanced planning of this early society. Inside the huts, replicas of everyday household objects allow you to imagine life within the community, revealing how these early inhabitants cooked, crafted tools, and maintained their homes with a remarkable level of sophistication for the era.

As you explore the site, you will see evidence of a tightly-knit community of about 300 people who lived through farming, hunting, and gathering. Archaeological discoveries include flint and bone tools, stone vessels, and intriguing anthropomorphic figurines that suggest the community practiced elaborate religious beliefs and funeral rituals, with some dead buried beneath the floors of their homes. This intimate connection between the living and the dead reflects the deep family ties and spiritual life of the settlers. The site also underscores a significant cultural link to the broader Near East, highlighting how early populations migrated and settled across regions.

Choirokoitia is not just about ancient ruins; it's a window into a prehistoric lifestyle surrounded by native Cypriot flora and fauna that have thrived since Neolithic times. The tranquil, scenic landscape provides a beautiful setting for visitors to take their time wandering through this open-air museum, absorbing the atmosphere where human history was first etched on the island.

The site is located approximately a 45-minute drive from Nicosia via the A1 highway, easily accessible by car or public transport, with buses running regularly from Larnaca and Limassol to the nearby area. Admission to Choirokoitia is free, and the site is open to visitors mostly during daylight hours, typically from early morning to early evening, although it's recommended to check current opening times before your visit. The site offers a visitor center with informative displays and guided tours that enhance the experience by providing deeper insights into the archaeological significance and daily life of the Neolithic settlers.

Exploring the Neolithic Settlement of Choirokoitia is a unique and enriching experience that transports you back over 8,000 years to the dawn of farming civilization in Cyprus. It is an essential visit for anyone interested in prehistoric culture, archaeology, or simply longing to connect with one of the island's oldest and most extraordinary heritage sites. The blend of history, architecture, spirituality, and the natural environment makes Choirokoitia a captivating destination that promises both education and wonder for every traveler.

Paphos

Paphos Archaeological Park (Tombs of the Kings, House of Dionysos)

Paphos Archaeological Park is one of the island's most captivating historical destinations and a UNESCO World Heritage site, offering visitors an extraordinary window into the ancient past of Cyprus. Situated near the bustling harbor of Paphos, this sprawling open-air complex features monuments and ruins that span from prehistoric times to the Middle Ages, with many of the most remarkable remains dating back to the Roman period when Paphos served as the island's capital.

Upon entering the park, you encounter an impressive array of archaeological treasures. Among the standout highlights are the Tombs of the Kings, a remarkable necropolis carved into the rock, dating back to the 4th century BC. Despite the name, no actual kings were buried here; rather, it served as a burial site for high-ranking officials and aristocrats. The scale of these underground tombs and their intricate facades create a hauntingly beautiful and evocative atmosphere, transporting visitors into the rituals and beliefs surrounding death in ancient Cyprus.

Another centerpiece of the park is the House of Dionysos, a large Roman villa famed for its stunning mosaic floors. These mosaics, among the best-preserved in the Mediterranean, vividly illustrate scenes from Greek mythology, particularly those related to Dionysos, the god of wine, along with depictions of mythical battles, animals, and hunting scenes that bring the art and stories of antiquity to life. Walking along elevated wooden pathways above these colorful mosaics, you can appreciate their intricate craftsmanship while imagining the luxurious life of a Roman noble in Paphos centuries ago.

Besides these main attractions, the park contains several other ancient villas with exquisite mosaics, such as the Houses of Theseus, Aion, and Orpheus, each showcasing unique mythological themes and artistic styles. Other notable monuments include the Roman Odeon, a small theatre from the 2nd century AD that still hosts cultural performances, and the Agora, the ancient marketplace surrounded by grand columns where once civic life thrived. Additionally, visitors can explore the remains of early Christian basilicas, the Asklepieion sanctuary, and medieval fortifications, all illustrating Paphos's long and diverse history.

The Archaeological Park is open daily, with hours adjusted seasonally, typically from early morning to early evening. The entrance fee is modest, making it accessible for all travelers eager to delve into Cyprus's ancient heritage. The park's location near the harbor and city center of Paphos makes it easy to reach on foot or by local transport, and ample signage and walkways help visitors navigate the expansive site comfortably.

It's an essential stop for anyone wanting to experience the grandeur of ancient Cyprus firsthand—whether wandering through the solemn tombs of the aristocracy or marveling at the vibrant mosaics that have survived millennia—and to appreciate Paphos's role as a cultural and political hub in antiquity. This fascinating site promises a deeply memorable experience combining beauty, history, and storytelling in one of Cyprus's most treasured archaeological parks.

Petra tou Romiou (Aphrodite's Rock)

Petra tou Romiou, widely known as Aphrodite's Rock, is one of Cyprus's most iconic and enchanting natural landmarks. Located on the southwest coast between Paphos and Limassol, this striking sea stack rises boldly from the turquoise Mediterranean waters, set against a backdrop of rugged coastline and lush scenery. The allure of Petra tou Romiou goes beyond its physical beauty: it is famously celebrated in Greek mythology as the mythical birthplace of Aphrodite, the ancient goddess of love and beauty, who is said to have emerged fully formed from the sea foam at this very spot. This legendary origin story imbues the area with a romantic and almost magical atmosphere, drawing travelers, honeymooners, and lovers of mythology and nature alike to experience this celebrated place.

When you visit Petra tou Romiou, you will encounter two adjoining beaches: one sandy and the other composed mostly of pebbles. The pebble beach, situated right next to the rock formation, offers unparalleled close-up views of the towering rock, but beware the water entrance can be tricky due to the pebbly sea bed and larger submerged rocks. The sandy beach provides a gentler access to the sea and more comfortable footing but is often met with stronger waves. The sea here is generally rough and is not recommended for swimming for safety reasons, but many visitors enjoy walking along the shore, taking photos, and simply soaking in the mesmerizing coastal vistas. Local legend holds that swimming around Aphrodite's Rock three times will grant blessings such as eternal youth, beauty, good fortune, fertility, and lasting love, which adds a layer of mystique to the visitor experience.

To reach Petra tou Romiou, you will find it easily accessible from the main coastal road connecting Paphos and Limassol. A large car park near the site offers convenient parking, and a pedestrian tunnel runs underneath the road to safely lead visitors down to the beach area. The walk from the parking area is pleasant, though the narrow tunnel en route may feel a bit confining for those with claustrophobia. Nearby, there are amenities including a café and a small shop catering to tourists. The rock itself is protected, so climbing on it is not permitted for safety and conservation reasons.

Petra tou Romiou is open to visitors year-round as a natural outdoor site with no entrance fee. The best time to visit is during daylight hours to fully appreciate the stunning views and to enjoy the coastal atmosphere. The surrounding area is also part of the Aphrodite Cultural Route, linking various sites associated with the goddess across Cyprus, making Petra tou Romiou a key highlight for cultural explorers. Although the rock has deep historical and mythological importance, the setting is very much a place to relax, stroll by the sea, and connect with the legendary spirit of love that Cyprus embodies.

Petra tou Romiou is more than just seeing a rock formation; it's immersing yourself in a captivating mix of natural wonder, ancient myth, and breathtaking Mediterranean beauty. This enchanting location offers a serene yet powerful connection to Cyprus's cultural heritage, making it a must-visit destination for anyone traveling the southern coast of the island. Whether you come for the views, the legends, or the peaceful walk along the shore, Aphrodite's Rock promises a memorable and meaningful experience.

Aphrodite's Baths

Aphrodite's Baths, located on the Akamas Peninsula near the town of Latchi and roughly an hour's drive from Paphos harbor, is a mesmerizing natural grotto steeped in ancient Greek mythology and surrounded by lush natural beauty. This enchanting spot is famed as the place where Aphrodite, the goddess of love and beauty, is said to have bathed in the cool, crystal-clear waters beneath the shade of an ancient fig tree. The small pool, fed by a natural spring flowing down the rocks, is wrapped in dense greenery and framed by twisted branches, creating a peaceful and almost magical atmosphere that captivates visitors from the moment they arrive.

The Baths of Aphrodite are not only a visual retreat but also a place woven deeply into local legend and spiritual heritage. According to myth, this was where Aphrodite met her lover Adonis, a tale that adds an air of romance and mystique to the site. The waters are reputed to have magical qualities, believed to grant beauty and fertility to those who bathe there, although swimming is no longer permitted to preserve the site's natural charm and tranquility. Surrounding the grotto is a botanical garden filled with indigenous plants and trees, inviting visitors to enjoy the diverse and serene flora as they stroll along paved trails.

For those eager to explore further, a scenic walking trail extends from the Baths, leading to an ancient oak tree said to be one of Aphrodite's favorite resting places. This trail splits into two longer routes named after the goddess and her lover, Adonis, each about five kilometers in length and showcasing remarkable Mediterranean coastal views along with opportunities to observe rare wildlife and plant species native to the Akamas Peninsula.

Visitors will find convenient amenities including a car park, a small café, and gift shops near the entrance. The site is accessible by car, making it ideal for a day trip from Paphos or Latchi. It is best to visit in the early morning or late afternoon to avoid crowds and to soak up the peacefulness of the surroundings. There is no entrance fee, and the natural setting invites visitors to relax, reflect, and connect with the timeless beauty and mythology of Cyprus.

Aphrodite's Baths offers a unique blend of natural splendor, ancient myth, and gentle adventure, making it a must-see attraction that leaves a lasting impression of romance and tranquility on all who experience it. Whether you come to absorb the legend, wander the botanical gardens, or hike the scenic trails, this spot on the Akamas Peninsula stands out as a magical highlight of any Cyprus journey.

Akamas Peninsula and Blue Lagoon

The Akamas Peninsula and Blue Lagoon together create one of the most breathtaking natural experiences in Cyprus, offering visitors a unique blend of wild scenery, crystal-clear waters, and ancient mythology.

The Akamas Peninsula is a largely untouched national park located on the island's rugged western coastline. It is a paradise for nature lovers and adventure seekers, with dramatic cliffs, dense pine forests, and secluded beaches. As you explore the area, you'll be rewarded with spectacular views over the Mediterranean Sea and a chance to see rare wildlife, including the famous loggerhead turtles that nest on Lara Beach during the summer months. The landscape is ideal for hiking, with trails like the Aphrodite Trail guiding you through scenic coastal paths and quiet coves.

One of the peninsula's jewels is the Baths of Aphrodite, a natural grotto surrounded by lush vegetation and a botanical garden, steeped in legend as the spot where the goddess of love supposedly bathed. The tranquil atmosphere of the baths provides a serene pause in your adventure, inviting you to connect with the myth and beauty of Cyprus.

Nestled nearby is the Blue Lagoon, a spectacularly clear and sheltered bay renowned for its striking turquoise waters and soft sandy bottom that beckons swimmers and snorkelers alike. Access to the Blue Lagoon is mainly by boat, with tours leaving from nearby Latchi harbor. These boat trips typically offer more than just transport; they create a full-day experience that combines swimming stops, breathtaking coastal scenery, and often a chance to enjoy local food or refreshments on board. Though the lagoon is stunning, facilities are very limited, so it's best to bring your own snorkeling gear, sun protection, and refreshments. The calm and shallow water here is perfect for relaxing swims and allows you to discover abundant marine life just beneath the surface.

For those who prefer land adventure, it's possible to hike from the Baths of Aphrodite to the Blue Lagoon, a rewarding trek of about an hour and a half. This trail winds through beautiful Mediterranean landscapes but requires preparation, as it's exposed, remote, and without shops or services along the way.

Ayia Napa And Protaras

Fig Tree Bay

Fig Tree Bay is one of the most popular and stunning beaches in Protaras, Cyprus. Known for its crystal-clear turquoise waters and soft, golden sand, the beach stretches about 500 meters and has earned the prestigious Blue Flag award for its cleanliness, water quality, and excellent public facilities. The bay is named after a solitary fig tree that stands at the headland, adding a charming natural touch to the picturesque setting.

This beach is family-friendly, with a large shallow area that makes swimming safe and enjoyable for children. Adventure seekers will also find plenty to do here, with water sports such as water-skiing, windsurfing, parasailing, and kayaking readily available. A small uninhabited islet is located just offshore, easily reachable by swimmers, offering a sheltered spot that helps keep the waters calm around the bay.

Facilities at Fig Tree Bay include sunbeds and umbrellas for hire, lifeguards on duty from April to October, and easy access with a municipal car park nearby. The beach is bordered by several restaurants, cafes, and bars, providing visitors with abundant options for dining and refreshments. In the late afternoon, the rocky promontory at the eastern end of the bay is a perfect spot to watch stunning sunsets.

Fig Tree Bay's combination of natural beauty, family-friendly atmosphere, aquatic activities, and amenities makes it a must-visit destination for anyone traveling to the Protaras area of Cyprus. Whether you want to relax on the sand, explore the nearby islet, or enjoy thrilling water sports, Fig Tree Bay offers a memorable seaside experience.

This beach is often lively, especially in peak tourist seasons, so arriving early can help secure good sunbeds and parking spaces.

If you are looking to stay nearby, there are plenty of villas and accommodation options offering close proximity to this beautiful beach, with some providing sea views and luxury amenities to enhance your stay in Cyprus.

The Ayia Napa Monastery

The Ayia Napa Monastery is a historic and spiritual landmark located in the heart of Ayia Napa, Cyprus. Dating back to the 15th century, during Venetian rule, it is a must-visit destination that offers a peaceful retreat from the bustling tourist town around it. The name "Ayia Napa" means "Saint of the Woods," reflecting the monastery's origins in a once-remote forested area.

The monastery is architecturally significant, featuring a blend of Gothic and Byzantine styles. It is characterized by stone-built structures surrounded by high walls and a beautiful cloistered courtyard with an elegant stone fountain popular among visitors. One of its unique features is an ancient sycamore tree at the entrance, believed to be over 600 years old, adding to the serene ambiance of the site.

At the core of the monastery lies a subterranean chapel, originally a cave where, according to legend, an icon of the Virgin Mary was discovered by a hunter around the 14th century. This cave became a sacred site, and eventually, the monastery was built around it with additional structures such as monastic cells and a mill funded by a Venetian noblewoman. The monastery served as a place of worship, refuge, and spiritual significance throughout its history, including during Ottoman rule when it was spared destruction and functioned as a cultural symbol.

Today, the Ayia Napa Monastery operates mostly as a museum with periodic religious services. Visitors can explore the tranquil gardens, historic buildings, and the small museum housing artifacts and religious icons that highlight the monastery's cultural and spiritual heritage. It is also a venue for religious festivals and local events, such as Greek Orthodox Easter celebrations and the Ayia Napa Festival in September.

Visiting the monastery offers a glimpse into Cyprus's rich religious tradition and architectural heritage, making it a serene and culturally enriching stop on any trip to Ayia Napa.

The monastery is open year-round to the public, providing a quiet oasis for contemplation and an opportunity to connect with the island's historical and spiritual roots

The Sculpture Park

The Sculpture Park in Ayia Napa is a captivating outdoor space where art and nature harmoniously come together. Located near the coast, this park features a striking collection of modern sculptures created by renowned Cypriot and international artists. As you wander along the well-maintained paths, you'll encounter a variety of works carved from marble, bronze, and other materials, each telling its own unique story.

Set against the backdrop of the Mediterranean Sea and lush greenery, the Sculpture Park provides a serene and inspiring atmosphere ideal for leisurely strolls, photography, and reflection. Many pieces explore themes of mythology, human emotion, and nature, making the park a vibrant cultural destination for art lovers and casual visitors alike.

Open year-round, the Sculpture Park is easily accessible and free to the public, making it a perfect stop during your visit to Ayia Napa. Whether you seek artistic inspiration or a peaceful place to relax by the seaside, this park offers a memorable experience blending creativity with the beauty of Cyprus's natural landscape.

The Thalassa Museum

The Thalassa Museum in Ayia Napa is a unique and modern museum dedicated entirely to the maritime heritage of Cyprus. It offers a fascinating journey through the island's deep connection with the sea, showcasing exhibits that span from prehistoric times to the present day. Named after the Greek word for "sea," the museum is the first of its kind in the Mediterranean region focused on the relationship between humans and the sea.

The museum building itself is an architectural marvel made from marble, onyx, wood, and metal, spread across three stories and subdivided into six levels. It offers a unique "bird's eye view" of the exhibits, which include a variety of display styles such as underwater-style showcases, modern cases, suspended exhibits, and more. Among the most captivating highlights is a full-scale replica of the famous 4th-century BC Kyrenia ship, an ancient Greek merchant vessel beautifully reconstructed and prominently displayed. Visitors can also explore fossils, sea life specimens millions of years old, archaeological treasures, and maritime artifacts spanning over 7,000 years of Cypriot history.

The museum combines education with interactive and multimedia displays, engaging visitors of all ages. It also has a marine life section in the basement, presenting fish, mammals, corals, shells, and fossils, some dating back over 100 million years. Beyond the exhibits, the facility includes an outdoor amphitheater for cultural performances, a multipurpose hall for lectures and workshops, a gift shop, and a café.

Conveniently located in central Ayia Napa, just a short walk from the beach and harbor, the Thalassa Museum is easily accessible and an excellent cultural alternative to the area's vibrant beach scene. It is open year-round, with extended hours during the summer months, and entrance fees are reasonable.

A Tour in the Thalassa Museum offers a captivating and educational experience that deepens your understanding of Cyprus's maritime traditions, natural history, and cultural development, making it a must-see for families, history enthusiasts, and any traveler seeking a meaningful cultural outing in Ayia Napa.

The Underwater Sculpture Park

The Underwater Sculpture Park near Ayia Napa offers an extraordinary fusion of art and marine life beneath the sea's surface. This unique attraction features an array of submerged sculptures crafted by talented artists, designed not only to provoke thought and creativity but also to serve as artificial reefs promoting biodiversity. As divers and snorkelers explore the site, they encounter evocative statues surrounded by flourishing marine ecosystems, where colorful fish and corals have made the artworks their home.

This place is situated just off the coast, this immersive experience combines the thrill of underwater exploration with cultural expression, providing a stunning contrast to traditional galleries. The sculptures, crafted from environmentally safe materials, encourage contemplation on themes such as humanity, nature, and transformation while enhancing marine habitat restoration efforts.

Very accessible primarily by boat and suitable for certified divers and adventurous snorkelers, the park offers a rare chance to engage with contemporary art in an underwater setting. Whether you are an art enthusiast, nature lover, or curious traveler, visiting the Underwater Sculpture Park promises a captivating journey into a serene underwater world where creativity meets conservation.

Nissi Beach

Nissi Beach in Ayia Napa is one of Cyprus's most famous and vibrant beaches, renowned for its beautiful golden sands and crystal-clear turquoise waters. The beach stretches about 500 meters within a cove sheltered by a small island called "Nissi" (meaning "island" in Greek), which visitors can easily reach on foot through shallow, knee-deep water. This natural feature creates calm, shallow waters perfect for swimming and safe for families, making it a favorite for both relaxation and water activities.

The atmosphere at Nissi Beach is lively and festive, particularly popular with young travelers, couples, and families alike. The beach is known for its energetic vibe, boosted by numerous beach bars and cafés that serve refreshing drinks and snacks from morning through evening, often accompanied by live DJs and music events during the busy summer months. It's a hotspot for beach parties and socializing, but also offers quieter spaces where visitors can simply enjoy the sun and sea.

In addition to sunbathing, visitors can enjoy a variety of water sports such as jet skiing, parasailing, paddleboarding, and snorkeling. Facilities include rentable sunbeds and umbrellas, public toilets, showers, and changing rooms, with lifeguards on duty during peak season, ensuring both convenience and safety.

Nissi Beach is easily accessible, located about 3 kilometers from Ayia Napa town center and well-served by car, taxi, bike, or public transport. There is ample parking nearby. The beach also holds a Blue Flag award, which guarantees high environmental and water quality standards.

Ideal visit times are spring and autumn for a quieter experience, while the summer months bring vibrant parties and full facilities. Weekdays tend to be less crowded than weekends. Whether you seek fun beach parties or relaxing Mediterranean charm, Nissi Beach offers a dynamic and unforgettable coastal experience in Cyprus.

The Troodos Mountains

Kykkos Monastery

The Troodos Mountains rise majestically in the heart of Cyprus, offering a refreshing respite from the coastal heat with their cool climate and verdant landscapes. This expansive mountain range is the largest on the island, characterized by rugged peaks, dense pine forests, and charming villages that seem frozen in time. As you wander through the winding roads and hidden trails, the Troodos Mountains reveal a treasure trove of natural beauty—crystal-clear streams, wildflowers, and panoramic vistas that stretch across the island. This region is a haven for hikers, nature lovers, and those seeking a tranquil escape immersed in the serenity of Cyprus's mountainous heartland.

Among the most distinguished landmarks nestled within this spectacular terrain is Kykkos Monastery, a symbol of spiritual devotion and Cypriot heritage. Founded in the late 11th century by Byzantine Emperor Alexios I Komnenos, Kykkos Monastery holds a prominent place in Cyprus's religious and cultural history. The monastery has endured centuries marked by fires and reconstructions, and while none of the original wooden structures remain today, the stone buildings that stand now echo the resilience and faith of generations past.

Its position is almost 1,300 meters above sea level on the slopes of the Troodos, Kykkos impresses visitors with its monumental Byzantine architecture, combining a fortress-like presence with intricate artistic details. The layout adapts ingeniously to the natural incline of the mountain, with multiple levels connected by stairways and galleries, giving the complex a labyrinthine charm. Inside, the monastery houses magnificent frescoes and mosaics that vividly depict religious scenes, showcasing the exceptional craftsmanship of Byzantine artists who contributed to its rich decoration.

The spiritual heartbeat of Kykkos Monastery is the revered Icon of the Virgin Mary, believed to have been painted by the Apostle Luke himself, according to tradition. This sacred icon is said to possess miraculous powers and draws pilgrims from around the world, imbuing the site with an aura of mysticism and reverence. The monastery also contains an ecclesiastical museum exhibiting an impressive collection of religious artifacts, including ancient manuscripts, vestments, and ceremonial objects that provide a window into the spiritual life and history of Cyprus.

Visiting Kykkos Monastery is more than a cultural excursion—it is a journey of contemplation and awe amid breathtaking mountain scenery. The monastery's setting offers both peace and grandeur, with views that stretch over verdant hills and valleys. Modest attire is required to respect the site's religious nature, and the journey to the monastery itself, often through winding mountain roads, adds to the sense of pilgrimage and discovery.

In essence, the Troodos Mountains and Kykkos Monastery together create an unforgettable experience where nature's magnificence meets profound spirituality and Byzantine artistry. This area invites you to immerse yourself in the tranquil rhythms of mountain life while exploring a cornerstone of Cypriot heritage that continues to inspire visitors with its deep history and timeless beauty. Whether you come for the hiking trails, the sacred icon, or simply the sublime vistas, the Troodos region with Kykkos at its heart promises a richly rewarding adventure.

Mount Olympus

Mount Olympus, also known as Chionistra, is the highest peak in Cyprus, towering at 1,952 meters (6,404 feet) in the Troodos Mountains. Located roughly in the center of the island, this majestic summit is part of the Troodos range, which is the largest mountain range in Cyprus and covers about a third of the island's area. The peak itself lies within the Limassol District, near the area of Platres.

Mount Olympus is notable not only for its elevation but also for its geological significance, being formed of ultramafic rock primarily serpentinized harzburgite, part of the Troodos ophiolite complex, which is an important and well-preserved geological formation. The summit area includes a British long-range radar installation, so the very top is restricted.

The climate at Mount Olympus is Mediterranean but cooler than the coastal regions, providing a refreshing contrast during Cyprus's hot summers. In winter, the mountain hosts Cyprus's only ski resort, operated by the Cyprus Ski Club, with several ski lifts and slopes catering to different skill levels—from beginners to advanced skiers. The ski areas include Sun Valley and North Face zones, offering T-bar lifts, chairlifts, and rope tows, making it the focal point for winter sports on the island.

In addition to winter activities, Mount Olympus and the surrounding Troodos Mountains are popular in warmer months for hiking, cycling, and nature exploration. The dense pine forests, cooler air, and panoramic views attract visitors seeking tranquility and natural beauty away from the coast. The mountain also holds historical significance: ancient geographer Strabo mentioned a temple dedicated to Aphrodite Acraea (Aphrodite of the Heights) located on one of its promontories, a sacred site from which women were traditionally barred.

Mount Olympus offers a rich blend of natural wonder, outdoor adventure, and cultural history, making it a must-see destination for anyone exploring Cyprus's diverse landscapes. Whether skiing in winter or hiking in summer, the mountain stands as a striking symbol of Cyprus's highest and most scenic elevations.

Omodos Village

Omodos Village, nestled in the Troodos Mountains of Cyprus, is a captivating destination known for its rich history, stunning natural surroundings, and vibrant cultural heritage. Located about 42 kilometers northwest of Limassol, the village sits near the west bank of the Chapotami River, at an altitude of approximately 810 meters, surrounded by towering mountain peaks including Afames, the tallest nearby peak.

Omodos's origins trace back to the late Byzantine era or the early period of Frankish rule in Cyprus. It emerged after the dissolution of the older Koupetra settlements on the opposite bank of the river. The village gradually formed around the Holy Cross Monastery, one of Cyprus's oldest and most important religious sites, said to house relics like a part of the Holy Cross and the Holy Rope connected to Christ. This monastery remains a central landmark, drawing numerous visitors with its spiritual and architectural significance.

The village is known for its large, picturesque stone-paved square, framed by traditional Cypriot houses and sycamore trees, perfect for leisurely walks, shopping for local crafts, or dining at tavernas serving authentic Cypriot cuisine. The atmosphere is charming year-round, with lively local festivals that celebrate the village's strong winemaking tradition—the annual wine festival is especially popular, showcasing local wines alongside traditional music and dance.

Omodos also has a deep connection to Cyprus's national history, playing an active role in the struggles for freedom throughout the 20th century, including the Greek revolution, both World Wars, and the EOKA liberation movement against British colonial rule. The village honors this heritage through museums and memorials dedicated to these pivotal events.

For travelers, Omodos offers not only cultural and historic allure but also breathtaking natural beauty, with vineyards, mountain trails, and scenic views that invite exploration. Accommodation options range from cozy guesthouses to boutique hotels, allowing visitors to immerse themselves fully in the tranquil mountain village lifestyle.

To point out, Omodos is a blend of history, faith, tradition, and natural splendor. Its tranquil setting, complemented by a welcoming community and cultural richness, makes it a memorable destination for those seeking to experience the heart of Cyprus beyond its coastal resorts. Whether visiting the monastery, enjoying local wines, or strolling through the scenic village square, Omodos promises an authentic and enriching Cypriot experience.

Wine Villages and Vineyards

The wine villages and vineyards of Cyprus, particularly those in the Krasochoria region near Limassol and along the southern slopes of the Troodos Mountains, form a renowned and historic viticultural area. Known locally as "Krasochoria," meaning "wine villages," this region encompasses about twenty traditional villages, each immersed in centuries of winemaking tradition and scenic beauty.

These villages have long been dedicated to cultivating vineyards, with many employing traditional methods handed down through generations. The area's dry climate and unique geology create ideal conditions for producing a variety of excellent wines, primarily from indigenous grape varieties such as Xynisteri (white) and Mavro (red). Alongside these local grapes, some international varieties like Cabernet Sauvignon, Grenache, Syrah, and Mataro are also cultivated here.

Among the notable villages are Omodos, Koilani, Lofou, Vouni, Arsos, and Vasa, each offering charming stone-paved streets, traditional architecture, and welcoming tavernas where visitors can enjoy local wines paired with Cypriot cuisine. Omodos, in particular, stands out with its historic monastery and annual wine festival celebrating the region's rich winemaking heritage.

Wineries in the Krasochoria region provide tasting tours where visitors can experience the full wine production process, from vineyard to glass. The local wines reflect the terroir's character, often exhibiting robust reds and crisp whites with distinctive Mediterranean flavors. The experience is enhanced by the picturesque landscapes and the warm hospitality of the village communities.

In addition to exploring the villages, travelers can enjoy cultural landmarks and beautiful hiking by the vineyards, making the wine route a blend of oenological discovery and authentic Cypriot rural life. Whether through lively wine festivals or quiet tasting rooms, the Krasochoria wine villages promise an immersive journey into Cyprus's deep-rooted winemaking tradition and stunning countryside.

Caledonia and Millomeris Waterfalls

Caledonia and Millomeris Waterfalls, nestled within the serene Troodos Mountains of Cyprus, are two of the island's most splendid natural highlights, offering visitors an immersive experience into the lush mountain wilderness.

Caledonia Waterfall plunges from a height of about 12 meters, making it one of the tallest waterfalls in Cyprus. Named by a Scottish expedition in the 19th century who were reminded of their homeland by the surrounding verdant vegetation, Caledonia cascades down amidst a backdrop of dense forest and colorful wildflowers. The waterfall is located roughly two kilometers north of the village of Pano Platres and can be reached via a scenic hiking trail approximately 3 kilometers long. The path follows the flowing Krios River, winding through shaded woodland filled with native flora and the melodic sounds of birdsong. The hike to the falls is moderately challenging, taking between 1.5 to 2.5 hours depending on pace, with some rocky and slippery sections where sturdy footwear is advised. For those seeking a shorter visit, a more direct 20-minute walk from the nearby Psilo Dendro Trout Farm provides easier access to the waterfall without the full trail. Many visitors enjoy standing beneath the cool cascade to refresh themselves and embrace the crisp mountain air, especially warm in the summer months. The area is magical year-round, with the lush landscape transforming beautifully across seasons.

Just a short drive or walk from the village of Platres lies Millomeris Waterfall, a smaller but equally enchanting cascade. Surrounded by moss-covered rocks and lush forest, Millomeris flows into a peaceful natural pool, perfect for relaxation and photography. The walk to Millomeris is gentler and shorter, around 45 to 60 minutes from the village, offering a tranquil woodland path lined with native plants. This waterfall is an ideal spot for picnicking and taking in the quiet atmosphere of the Troodos wilderness.

Both waterfalls reflect the rich natural heritage of the Troodos region and provide refreshing escapes from Cyprus's coastal heat. They are popular with hikers, families, and nature lovers seeking a peaceful day surrounded by pristine mountain scenery. Adequate footwear, water, and sun protection are recommended, especially during summer hikes.

Exploring Caledonia and Millomeris Waterfalls means experiencing the best of Cyprus's mountainous landscapes—towering cascades, vibrant forests, and scenic trails weaving through nature's splendor. These gems offer peaceful retreats and memorable moments amid the tranquil beauty of the Troodos Mountains.

ACTIVITIES AND EXPERIENCES

Water Sports and Diving

South Cyprus is a dream for water lovers. With its long summer season, warm Mediterranean waters, and calm sea conditions, it's no surprise that water sports and diving are some of the most popular activities on the island. Whether you're an adrenaline-seeker looking to ride the waves or someone who simply wants to glide over the water in peace, there's something here for every type of traveler. The coastline is dotted with beautiful beaches, rocky coves, and hidden bays — all offering perfect settings for jet skiing, parasailing, kayaking, snorkeling, paddleboarding, and some of the best diving in the Mediterranean.

Water sports are available in most major beach towns, but each area has its own unique charm. Protaras and Ayia Napa are known for their action-packed offerings, while Paphos and Limassol offer a more laid-back approach. The variety is endless, but the heart of it all is the sea itself — clear, blue, and full of life.

In Protaras and Ayia Napa, you'll find almost every water sport imaginable. You can rent jet skis and zoom across the waves, take a banana boat ride with friends for some serious laughter, or go parasailing and catch breathtaking views of the coastline from above. If you're feeling adventurous, try flyboarding, where jets of water lift you into the air in a balancing act that feels like something straight out of a superhero movie.

For a calmer experience, stand-up paddleboarding (SUP) and sea kayaking are excellent options, especially in the early morning when the sea is calm. You can paddle into small caves and explore hidden corners of the coastline you can't reach by foot. Some operators offer guided SUP tours during sunrise or sunset — a truly peaceful way to start or end your day.

Diving, however, is where South Cyprus truly shines. The island is home to the famous Zenobia wreck near Larnaca — a massive Swedish ferry that sank on her maiden voyage in 1980. Today, it's considered one of the top wreck dives in the world. The ship lies on her side at depths ranging from 16 to 42 meters, making it accessible for both intermediate and experienced divers. Exploring the cargo decks, cabins, and the sheer scale of the wreck is an unforgettable experience.

Beyond Zenobia, the Akrotiri Fish Reserve near Limassol and the caves and reefs around Cape Greco offer exciting dives for all levels. You can expect to see groupers, sea bream, octopus, moray eels, and sometimes even turtles or rays. Snorkelers will enjoy the clear, shallow waters around Fig Tree Bay or Konnos Bay, where you can easily spot colorful fish and underwater rock formations.

Water sports are widely available from April to November, with peak activity during the summer months from June through September. Most beachside resorts and kiosks offer rentals and sessions daily from around 9:00 AM until 6:00 PM, though hours can vary slightly depending on the season and location. Prices depend on the activity, but you can expect to pay around €25–€35 for a 15-minute jet ski session, €20–€30 for parasailing, and around €10–€15 for kayaking or paddleboard rental per hour.

If you're interested in diving, you'll find certified dive centers in every major town — Larnaca, Limassol, Paphos, Ayia Napa, and Protaras. A standard introductory dive (Discover Scuba) usually starts at around €60–€80, which includes equipment and instructor guidance. For certified divers, dives to the Zenobia wreck start at around €90–€120 depending on the dive shop and whether equipment rental is needed. Most centers also offer certification courses from beginner (Open Water) to advanced levels.

Safety is a priority with most operators, and many are affiliated with recognized organizations like PADI or SSI. Always choose licensed, reputable companies and never hesitate to ask about their safety measures, instructors, and insurance.

Some areas like Cape Greco and certain protected coves are part of national parks or marine reserves, and while water activities are still allowed, respect for local rules and environmental guidelines is essential. Avoid touching marine life, collecting shells or coral, and be sure to use reef-safe sunscreen.

If you're bringing your own gear — especially for snorkeling — you'll have even more freedom to explore, but keep in mind that some areas have strong currents or boat traffic. Always check local advice, and never swim or dive alone.

Hiking and Nature Trails

South Cyprus isn't just about golden beaches and ancient ruins — it's also a land of dramatic landscapes, rolling mountains, lush forests, and scenic trails that stretch across hillsides, gorges, and coastlines. Hiking here is more than just a way to stretch your legs; it's an invitation to slow down and experience the natural beauty, history, and serenity that this island offers beyond the tourist hotspots. Whether you're looking for a quiet morning walk with sea views or a more challenging mountain adventure, South Cyprus delivers trails for every level and every kind of traveler.

The Troodos Mountains, Cape Greco National Forest Park, and the Akamas Peninsula are the three major hiking regions that offer some of the best walking experiences in the country. Each has its own character — from shady pine forests and gushing waterfalls to coastal cliffs and ancient stone paths, some dating back centuries. Along the way, you'll encounter wildflowers, butterflies, goats, and the occasional old chapel or village that feels untouched by time.

One of the most rewarding hikes is the **Caledonia Trail** in the Troodos Mountains. This cool, shaded path follows a stream and winds through tall pines and plane trees, leading you to the picturesque Caledonia Waterfall — one of the highest in Cyprus. It's especially beautiful in spring and early summer when the flow is strong and the surrounding vegetation is lush and green. The trail is about 3 kilometers long and moderately easy, with spots to rest, enjoy the sound of rushing water, and take in the scent of fresh earth and forest.

Another favorite is the **Aphrodite Trail** in the Akamas Peninsula, which starts at the Baths of Aphrodite and climbs high above the sea to offer stunning views over the coastline. The full loop is around 7.5 kilometers, and while the uphill sections can be challenging, the rewards are unforgettable — panoramic views, ancient ruins, wild herbs growing underfoot, and long stretches of silence broken only by the sound of the breeze and distant waves. Along this trail, you'll also pass the ruins of a medieval tower and, on clear days, see all the way to the tip of the peninsula.

For those who prefer sea views with their steps, the **Cape Greco National Forest Park** near Ayia Napa offers gentle coastal trails with breathtaking scenery. The trails here are well-marked and relatively flat, making them perfect for families or casual walkers. You'll pass limestone cliffs, rock formations, sea caves, and even the famous natural arch known as the "Bridge of Lovers." There's also a small church perched above the sea and several shaded picnic areas to stop for a rest. The light here is magical at sunrise and sunset, casting golden hues over the rock and sea.

If you're looking for something quieter and more off-the-beaten-path, try the **Millomeris Waterfall Trail** near Platres village. It's a short but beautiful hike through forest and rock, ending in a narrow canyon with a waterfall that drops into a cold, clear pool. This one is perfect for a quick afternoon escape, especially on a hot day.

For longer hikes, the **Atalante Trail** in Troodos is a 14-kilometer loop that circles Mount Olympus, the highest point in Cyprus. This trail is rich with panoramic views and shaded by black pine and juniper trees. It's long but not technically difficult, making it suitable for active travelers looking for an immersive nature experience. On a clear day, you can see all the way to the sea on both the north and south sides of the island.

Most hiking trails in South Cyprus are open year-round, though spring (March to May) and autumn (September to November) offer the best conditions — mild weather, fewer crowds, and blooming landscapes. Summer hikes are still possible, but it's essential to go early in the morning or late in the afternoon to avoid the midday heat, especially on open, coastal trails. Winters can bring snow in the higher elevations of the Troodos Mountains, which adds a magical layer to certain paths but may also make them slippery or temporarily inaccessible.

Entrance to national parks and nature trails is free, including Caledonia, Cape Greco, and the Akamas trails. Parking is usually available near trailheads, but it can fill up quickly on weekends and holidays, so arriving early is wise. Most trails are well-marked with signs in both Greek and English, though it's always a good idea to carry a map or use a GPS app like AllTrails or Maps.me for added security, especially on longer routes.

Facilities vary depending on the location. The Caledonia and Millomeris trails have nearby cafés and public restrooms in Platres village, while Cape Greco and Akamas are more remote, with basic or no services along the trails. Carry water, sunscreen, snacks, and a hat — and wear proper footwear. Even short trails can have uneven or rocky paths that are slippery when wet. Cell phone coverage may drop in more remote areas, so let someone know where you're going if you're hiking alone.

Guided hikes are available through local tour operators if you'd prefer a structured experience with background stories and historical insights. These guides are especially useful in places like Akamas, where ancient sites and mythological landmarks are scattered throughout the region and often missed by casual walkers.

Finally, remember that South Cyprus is home to fragile ecosystems, especially in protected areas like the Akamas Peninsula. Stay on marked paths, avoid picking flowers or disturbing wildlife, and carry your rubbish out with you. Hiking here is not just an activity — it's a way to connect with the land, history, and quiet beauty of Cyprus, and it's best enjoyed with respect and care.

Wine Tasting and Vineyard Tours

South Cyprus has been making wine for over 5,000 years — and you can taste that rich, ancient tradition in every glass. With its sunny climate, fertile soil, and time-honored techniques passed down through generations, the region produces some of the most unique and characterful wines in the Mediterranean. Tucked into the hills of the Troodos Mountains and beyond are countless small vineyards and family-run wineries where tradition meets passion — and where every visit feels like you're stepping into someone's story.

Wine tasting in Cyprus isn't just about sipping wine; it's about slowing down and enjoying the countryside, the conversation, and the quiet luxury of vineyard life. Whether you're a complete beginner or a dedicated wine enthusiast, you'll find that Cyprus' wine culture is welcoming, laid-back, and full of surprising flavors. From the legendary Commandaria — one of the world's oldest named wines — to crisp Xynisteri whites and full-bodied Maratheftiko reds, there's something here for every palate.

Start your wine journey in the **Krasochoria**, or "Wine Villages," nestled in the foothills of the Troodos Mountains. This group of picturesque villages includes Omodos, Koilani, Vasa, Arsos, and several others, each with its own character and winemaking traditions. These villages are dotted with small, often family-run wineries where you can walk through the vineyards, visit stone cellars, and taste wines straight from the source.

Omodos is perhaps the most popular and well-preserved wine village. It offers a mix of cultural charm, beautiful architecture, and several tasting rooms. You can explore cobblestone streets, visit the 17th-century Holy Cross Monastery, and then settle into a courtyard with a glass of dry white or sweet red as the village hums quietly around you. Many wineries here also serve meze —

traditional Cypriot small plates — which perfectly complement the wine and turn a tasting into a full, leisurely meal.

If you're looking for a more in-depth experience, many vineyards offer guided tours that walk you through the entire winemaking process, from grape to glass. You'll learn about local grape varieties like Mavro and Xynisteri, see how modern equipment blends with traditional clay jars and oak barrels, and chat with winemakers who will proudly tell you about their family's history and philosophy. Some even let you help with the harvest if you visit during grape-picking season in late summer.

In **Limassol's wine-producing region**, you'll find larger estates with beautifully designed tasting rooms and terraces that overlook endless rows of vines. Some, like those in Agios Amvrosios and Pachna, focus on organic methods and experimental blends, offering a different spin on classic Cypriot wine culture. Others offer vertical tastings — sampling different vintages of the same wine — for those who want to go deeper.

Don't miss out on trying **Commandaria**, the sweet, fortified wine that Cyprus is famous for. It has an almost mythical history, said to be favored by Crusaders and kings, and is made from sun-dried grapes aged in oak barrels. Even if you're not usually a fan of dessert wines, the balance of rich fruit and spice in a good Commandaria is hard to resist.

For a different experience, some wineries offer **wine and art pairings**, live music events, or cooking classes alongside the tastings, turning your visit into a relaxed, cultural outing. Many are set in gorgeous locations, surrounded by gardens, vineyards, and mountain views, making them ideal for photos or simply soaking up the scenery.

Most wineries in South Cyprus are open year-round, with the busiest seasons being spring, summer, and early autumn. Many small vineyards welcome visitors without a reservation, especially in popular wine villages like Omodos and Koilani, but calling ahead is always a good idea if you're planning to visit a specific estate or want a private tour. Some wineries close on Sundays or during harvest, so checking in advance saves you a wasted trip.

Tasting fees vary, but most places offer a generous selection for €5–€10 per person, often waived if you purchase a bottle or two. Guided tours typically cost between €10 and €20, depending on the experience and whether food is included. Most tastings include 3 to 6 wines, and it's common to be offered snacks like olives, bread, or cheese to cleanse your palate between sips.

Many of the best wineries are located along winding mountain roads, so if you're driving, it's best to designate a sober driver or join a wine tour. Several companies offer half-day or full-day guided wine tours that include transportation, winery visits, and local food stops, making it a safe and convenient way to explore. If you're staying in Limassol, Paphos, or Larnaca, most tours will pick you up directly from your hotel.

Temperatures in the mountains can be cooler than the coast, so bring a light jacket if you're visiting in spring or fall. Comfortable shoes are a must, especially if your tour includes vineyard walks or cobbled village streets.

Lastly, most wineries sell their bottles on-site at very reasonable prices, and many offer shipping options if you want to send a few favorites home. It's the perfect souvenir — not just a bottle of wine, but a taste of the land, the sun, and the stories you've just experienced.

Cultural Festivals and Events

South Cyprus is not just a place of beautiful beaches and historic ruins — it's a living, breathing culture that loves to celebrate. Festivals and events here are full of color, tradition, music, food, and community spirit. Whether it's a religious celebration passed down for generations, a harvest festival in a mountain village, or a modern celebration of art and film, the island knows how to throw a party. Attending a local festival offers travelers a deeper look at the soul of Cyprus — where ancient roots meet lively rhythms and everyone, local or visitor, is welcome to join in.

Throughout the year, there are festivals large and small, spread across cities, towns, and tiny villages. From the massive Carnival in Limassol to quiet Easter processions in mountain communities, each one offers something unique — and they're some of the most unforgettable experiences a traveler can have here.

If you're visiting in February or March, you might be lucky enough to catch **Limassol Carnival**, the biggest and most exciting festival on the island. This 11-day celebration is Cyprus' answer to Mardi Gras, complete with parades, costumes, dancing, live music, and street food. The whole city gets involved — families, schools, and performers take to the streets in full costume, and the energy is contagious. The final Grand Parade is a sight to behold, with floats, dancers, confetti, and a sea of happy faces filling the city's avenues. It's a playful, joyous experience that brings everyone together.

Spring brings the **Flower Festival**, known locally as Anthestiria. Celebrated in early May in towns like Limassol and Larnaca, this event honors the rebirth of nature and the arrival of spring. Streets are decorated with floral floats, fresh blossoms, and vibrant displays. The air smells of jasmine and roses, and the festive mood is gentle, full of music, families strolling, and people handing out flowers to passersby. It's a great time to witness local pride and craftsmanship — and take plenty of colorful photos.

In summer, things heat up both temperature-wise and culturally. July and August are packed with events, including the **Pafos Aphrodite Festival**, an internationally acclaimed open-air opera held each year in front of the medieval castle by the harbor. Sitting under the stars, listening to world-class performances with the sea behind you is a magical, spine-tingling experience, whether you're a seasoned opera lover or just curious. Book your tickets early, as the event draws people from all over the world.

Also during summer is the **Limassol Wine Festival**, usually held in late August or early September. This is a lively celebration of Cypriot wine culture — with music, dancing, and, of course, endless wine tastings. It's hosted in the Municipal Gardens of Limassol, and you'll find local wineries pouring samples of their best reds and whites, traditional food stalls, folk dancing, and even grape-stomping contests for kids and adults alike. It's joyful, relaxed, and a perfect way to sample the best of Cyprus without needing to tour every vineyard yourself.

Easter in Cyprus, usually in April, is one of the most deeply felt and spiritually important times of the year. From Good Friday processions with candles and church bells to Easter Sunday feasts, the whole week is filled with rituals, tradition, and a sense of togetherness. If you're in a village during Easter, you may be invited to join a family for roast lamb, flaounes (cheese-filled pastries), and a long, celebratory meal that often stretches late into the afternoon. Experiencing Easter here is like stepping into a different pace of life — one that values tradition, food, family, and shared time.

Another standout is **Kataklysmos**, or the Festival of the Flood, celebrated in coastal towns like Larnaca and Ayia Napa around Pentecost (usually in June). Rooted in both Christian and ancient

Greek traditions, it's a water-themed celebration featuring games, music, dancing, and boat races. Families gather by the sea, and the air is filled with laughter, sea breeze, and the sound of splashing water from games and traditions meant to "cleanse" and bless.

For those who prefer modern art and music, **Cyprus Film Days**, the **Cyprus International Food Festival**, and various jazz and electronic music events offer a more contemporary take on island culture. These events, held mainly in cities like Nicosia, Limassol, and Paphos, attract international artists and performers, and bring together people from all walks of life to celebrate creativity, diversity, and innovation.

Festival schedules vary slightly each year depending on the religious calendar and planning decisions by local municipalities. It's always best to check dates in advance if you're planning your trip around a specific event. Tourist offices in each town often publish festival calendars, and hotels usually provide updates as well. Many of the larger festivals — like Limassol Carnival or the Wine Festival — have dedicated websites and social media pages with up-to-date information.

Entrance fees depend on the festival. Many events, such as village celebrations, Kataklysmos, and the Flower Festival, are free and open to the public. Others, like the Aphrodite Opera Festival or certain performances during Easter, may require tickets, which typically range from €10 to €50 depending on the seat and event. Wine Festival entry is usually around €5–€10 and often includes a commemorative glass and unlimited tastings.

Transportation during festival times can be busy, especially in the cities. Parking fills up quickly, and some roads may be closed for parades or pedestrian zones. Plan to arrive early or use public transport or taxis when possible. In small villages, parking is often informal — just follow the crowd and local advice.

As for what to wear: festivals in Cyprus are casual and relaxed, but always consider the season. Summers are hot, so light clothing, comfortable shoes, and a sun hat are essential. Evenings, especially in the mountains or by the sea, can cool down slightly, so bring a light layer if you're attending a night event. During religious festivals like Easter, modest clothing is recommended if you're attending church services or joining a procession.

Above all, bring your curiosity and your camera. But more importantly, bring a willingness to join in. Say yes when someone hands you a flower or a glass of wine. Dance if the music moves you. Smile when the parade passes by. Because in South Cyprus, festivals aren't just performances — they're moments of shared joy, and every visitor is invited.

Nightlife and Entertainment

South Cyprus may greet you with quiet beaches and ancient ruins by day, but once the sun dips below the horizon, the island pulses with energy. Nightlife here is as varied as the landscape — from wild beach parties and buzzing clubs to elegant cocktail lounges, casual tavern evenings, and intimate live music venues tucked into stone alleys. Whether you're looking to dance until dawn, sip wine under fairy lights, or simply enjoy a laid-back night with locals, there's something here for every mood and every traveler.

The island's nightlife hotspots are mostly concentrated in a few key areas: Ayia Napa, Limassol, Larnaca, and Paphos. Each city has its own flavor — Ayia Napa is wild and youthful, Limassol is stylish and cosmopolitan, Larnaca blends the casual with the traditional, and Paphos offers a charming mix of seafront calm and party buzz. But no matter where you are, you'll find the warm, open-armed spirit that makes Cypriot nights feel like a celebration of life.

Start with the most famous: **Ayia Napa**. This once-quiet fishing village is now the party capital of the island and one of the top nightlife destinations in Europe. The square at the heart of the town is surrounded by dozens of clubs, bars, and lounges, each with its own style and vibe. You can start your night with pre-drinks at a low-key pub, then move into dance clubs that don't really start heating up until after midnight. Names like Castle Club and Soho are known across Europe, drawing top DJs, themed parties, and crowds that dance until the sun rises.

But Ayia Napa isn't all electronic beats and glitter cannons. There are also cozy cocktail bars, beachfront lounges where you can watch fire shows, and beach clubs that host sunset parties with live DJs, champagne sprays, and a view that's pure magic. Even if you're not a clubber, the energy here is infectious — and everyone is welcome.

For a more sophisticated scene, head to **Limassol**. This city has polished its nightlife into something sleek and elegant. The marina and Old Town are lined with chic wine bars, rooftop lounges, speakeasies, and restaurants that turn into music-filled social hubs after dinner. You can sip Cypriot wine while listening to soft jazz, dance to house beats on a rooftop overlooking the sea, or enjoy craft cocktails in candle-lit corners that feel like a secret. Weekends are lively, but the scene here is more about style and atmosphere than full-blown chaos.

Larnaca offers a nice middle ground — a mix of beach bars, local tavern nights, and friendly pubs. The Finikoudes Promenade comes alive after sunset, with live music, bustling terraces, and street performers adding color to the scene. You can walk with an ice cream, find a seat by the sea, or settle into a bar for a relaxed night with good drinks and better company. For a more local feel, head to the backstreets and explore the tiny bars hidden behind old wooden doors — often filled with locals playing cards or singing along to traditional music.

Paphos is more laid-back, but don't let that fool you — there's still plenty of action after dark. The harbor area is great for a romantic dinner followed by a quiet drink with sea views, while the bar street near Kato Paphos offers livelier options for those who want to stay out late. In the summer, open-air bars set up along the coast, complete with bean bags, fairy lights, and the sound of waves blending with music. It's a softer kind of nightlife, but no less enjoyable — especially if you love good wine, stargazing, and friendly vibes.

Beyond the usual party spots, Cyprus also loves **live music and performance**. Traditional music nights in villages are a must-see — with locals playing the violin-like "lyra," dancers in traditional dress, and hearty communal meals. In bigger cities, you'll find jazz bars, rock gigs, and cultural centers hosting theatre, poetry, and dance. Nicosia, although technically just outside of South Cyprus' border division, is also worth mentioning for those looking for indie concerts, film screenings, and late-night cafés with a creative twist.

Most bars and lounges open by early evening, around 6:00 PM or 7:00 PM, though the real nightlife usually starts picking up after 10:00 PM. Clubs in Ayia Napa and Limassol often don't hit full energy until midnight and stay open until 4:00 AM or later. During summer months — especially July and August — these venues are packed and buzzing every night of the week, while in the cooler months, weekends are your best bet for finding a crowd.

There is usually no entrance fee for bars and most lounges, but clubs may charge a cover, especially for special DJ nights or big events. This can range from €10 to €20 and may include a drink. Dress codes are generally relaxed, but in higher-end venues in Limassol or private parties in Ayia Napa, it's best to dress smart-casual. Flip-flops and beachwear are fine during the day, but most places expect a little more effort after sunset.

If you're planning to drink, taxis are widely available and relatively inexpensive in most cities. In tourist hubs, it's easy to flag one down or find a stand near clubs and beach bars. However, they can get scarce late at night in remote areas or villages, so it's a good idea to book in advance if you're outside the main towns.

As always, keep an eye on your belongings in busy places, and stay hydrated — summer nights can be hot, and with all the dancing and drinking, it's easy to forget how much sun you've already soaked up that day. Drink responsibly, look out for your friends, and enjoy the island's hospitality — because Cyprus nightlife isn't about exclusivity, it's about togetherness. Everyone's welcome, and every night holds the chance for new music, new friends, and stories you'll be telling long after your trip ends.

Shopping: Markets and Boutiques

Shopping in South Cyprus is more than just a way to pass the time — it's a cultural experience in itself. From vibrant local markets and family-run workshops to trendy boutiques and charming souvenir shops, every corner of the island offers a chance to discover something unique. The island's shopping scene blends the traditional with the modern, allowing travelers to take home not only handmade treasures and local delicacies, but also stylish fashion, artisanal crafts, and memories woven into fabric, taste, and scent.

Whether you're wandering through the winding streets of old towns, browsing open-air stalls on a sunny morning, or stepping into modern boutiques with sleek displays, the experience feels personal. Many sellers are the artists or makers themselves, eager to share their story and passion. It's a refreshing break from mass-produced souvenirs and a wonderful way to support local creators.

For travelers looking for a truly authentic shopping experience, the best place to begin is at a **local market**. One of the most popular is the **Municipal Market in Limassol**, known locally as the "Pantopoleio." This covered market buzzes with life — from fresh fruits and vegetables to herbs, cheeses, olives, dried fruits, local wines, and handmade goods. Walking through it feels like stepping into the daily life of the city, with the rich scent of spices in the air and friendly vendors ready to hand you a sample of carob syrup or freshly roasted nuts. It's a perfect place to pick up edible souvenirs, and also just to feel the heartbeat of the town.

In **Nicosia's old city**, Ledra and Onasagorou Streets are home to a delightful mix of traditional and modern shops. You can find handcrafted leather goods, lace, Cypriot pottery, woven baskets, natural cosmetics made with olive oil and herbs, and even reimagined versions of traditional designs presented with a modern twist. This area also has independent bookstores, art galleries, and vintage shops, ideal for those looking to bring something thoughtful and original back home.

The **village of Lefkara** deserves a special mention — known internationally for its lace-making, called "Lefkaritika." This delicate craft has been practiced here for centuries, and was even admired by Leonardo da Vinci, who is said to have taken a piece back to Italy. Today, you can watch elderly women sit in the doorways of their homes, lacework in hand, chatting with passersby while they work. Shops throughout the village sell tablecloths, doilies, and linen embroidered with detailed, timeless patterns. Alongside the lace, you'll also find fine silverwork, another craft the village is famous for.

In the Troodos mountain villages, small shops sell **locally made wine, honey, jams, herbs, and handmade soaps**. These products are often made in tiny batches with generations of know-how behind them. Many shops will let you taste the jams or try out the oils, and it's a beautiful way to connect with the land through flavor and scent.

For a more modern shopping fix, **Limassol's My Mall** or **Nicosia's The Mall of Cyprus** provide large, air-conditioned centers with international brands, designer fashion, cosmetics, electronics, and dining options. While they're more commercial in nature, they offer a contrast to the island's rustic charm and provide a good stop for those seeking a mix of convenience and variety.

Jewelry lovers will enjoy exploring shops around **Paphos Harbor**, where goldsmiths and silversmiths create elegant pieces inspired by ancient designs. Many items draw from Byzantine and Hellenistic motifs, and you'll often find necklaces, rings, and bracelets that blend traditional beauty with modern style.

And then there are the **seasonal craft fairs and pop-up markets**, especially around Christmas and Easter, where artisans from across the island showcase their handmade products. These temporary events are full of joy, color, and creativity, and they're a fantastic way to connect directly with makers.

Opening hours for shops and markets in South Cyprus vary by location and season. In general, most **small shops and boutiques open around 9:00 AM and close between 6:00 PM and 7:00 PM**, with a lunch break in the middle of the day — often between 1:00 PM and 3:00 PM, especially in smaller towns or villages. On Wednesdays and Saturdays, many shops close earlier, and Sundays are generally a rest day for local businesses, though this doesn't apply to shops in tourist-heavy areas, which often stay open all week.

Major shopping malls usually **stay open from 10:00 AM to 8:00 PM**, and remain open on Sundays and public holidays.

Cash is widely accepted in markets and village shops, though many places also accept cards. Still, it's a good idea to carry some cash — especially in small villages or rural areas. Bargaining isn't common in boutiques, but in markets or with local artisans, there's often a bit of flexibility, especially if you're buying more than one item.

VAT refunds may be available for non-EU residents on purchases over a certain amount, so keep your receipts and ask the shop if they participate in the refund scheme. Most airports have a VAT refund counter where you can process your paperwork before departure.

When buying food or beauty products, check for **production dates and ingredients** — Cyprus has strict standards, but it's always wise to make sure products are fresh and naturally made. If you're buying lace or handcrafted items, don't be afraid to ask how they were made. Many shopkeepers are proud of their work and happy to tell you the story behind it — and that story becomes part of the souvenir.

Ultimately, shopping in South Cyprus is about slowing down, taking your time, and connecting with the place. Whether you're walking through a bustling city street or a quiet mountain village, what you take home isn't just a product — it's a piece of the island's heart.

Culinary Delights: Where to Eat

Food in South Cyprus is more than just nourishment — it's culture, community, and celebration all served on a plate. Every meal here tells a story, one flavored with Mediterranean sun, mountain herbs, local olive oil, and centuries of tradition. Whether you're dining by the sea, perched in a village taverna, or sharing a homemade meal with locals, you'll quickly realize that Cypriot cuisine isn't just delicious — it's deeply personal.

The culinary scene across South Cyprus is a beautiful blend of tradition and modern flair. Old recipes passed down through generations are still the backbone of village kitchens, while young chefs in the cities bring creative twists to local ingredients. And the best part? You don't need to search too hard to eat well here. Good food finds you — in tiny bakeries, roadside grills, bustling city markets, and elegant restaurants with white linen tables and sea views.

Start your food adventure with the **meze** — not just a meal, but a ritual. A proper Cypriot meze can feature over twenty small dishes served one after the other, giving you a full taste of the island's rich variety. Expect creamy hummus, tangy tzatziki, fresh village salad topped with olives and feta, spicy sausages called "sheftalia," grilled halloumi, slow-cooked lamb, and fragrant stews. Meze is best enjoyed slowly, with good company and a local wine or cold beer, under warm lights and the soft hum of conversation.

In coastal towns like **Larnaca, Limassol, and Paphos**, seafood reigns supreme. You'll find restaurants where the catch of the day is displayed on ice for you to choose — sea bass, red mullet, calamari, octopus, and shrimp, all grilled or baked to perfection. Pair it with a glass of white Xynisteri wine and a view of the sunset over the Mediterranean, and you've got a memory that lasts longer than any photo.

Head inland and you'll discover the hearty, soul-warming food of the villages. In **Troodos** or small towns like **Omodos** and **Arsos**, you'll find clay pot stews like "kleftiko" — lamb slow-baked until it falls apart — and "afelia," pork marinated in red wine and coriander. Bread is often fresh-baked and served warm, the olives are picked nearby, and every dish carries a sense of pride. These meals are usually served in humble, family-run taverns where the owner might be your waiter, your cook, and your storyteller all in one.

Don't miss out on **street food and casual eats** either. In city centers, you'll find wraps of souvlaki — skewered meat wrapped in warm pita with salad and creamy sauces — sold from tiny shops and food trucks. **Loukoumades**, the golden fried dough balls soaked in honey or syrup, make the perfect sweet snack, especially when sprinkled with cinnamon and crushed nuts.

Bakeries are another must-visit. Open from early morning, they offer everything from warm cheese pastries called **flaounes** and sesame-covered bread rings to seasonal sweets like **melomakarona** — honey-drenched cookies often served around Christmas. Many bakeries double as small cafés where you can grab a Cypriot coffee and watch the town wake up.

For those who love modern dining, cities like **Nicosia and Limassol** are full of stylish bistros, fusion kitchens, and international restaurants that bring global flavors to local ingredients. You'll find everything from vegan options and tapas bars to gourmet takes on traditional recipes. Fine dining here still keeps its Cypriot soul — warm hospitality, generous portions, and deep respect for the land.

Meal times in Cyprus are relaxed and often run later than in other parts of Europe. Lunch is typically enjoyed between **1:00 PM and 3:00 PM**, while dinner often starts around **8:00 PM or later**, especially in summer. Most restaurants stay open until **11:00 PM**

or midnight, and many cafés and bakeries open early — sometimes as early as **6:30 AM** — to serve breakfast, coffee, and pastries.

Tipping is not mandatory but always appreciated. Leaving **5% to 10%** of the bill is a common way to show gratitude for good service. In smaller places, tipping in coins or simply rounding up the bill is perfectly fine.

Reservations are not usually necessary in tavernas or casual spots, especially during the day, but for dinner in popular restaurants — particularly in Limassol, Ayia Napa, or near the coast during high season — it's a good idea to book ahead. Many places now take reservations via phone, social media, or even apps.

Menus are typically available in both **Greek and English**, and staff in tourist areas usually speak enough English to help you choose. Many restaurants also accommodate dietary preferences, offering vegetarian, gluten-free, and even vegan dishes — though it's always helpful to ask clearly, as traditional dishes may contain dairy or meat broth.

Lastly, if you're in Cyprus during a **religious holiday or festival**, don't be surprised if restaurants feature special seasonal dishes — like lamb feasts at Easter or fasting-friendly vegan menus during Lent. These traditions give a unique glimpse into the spiritual and cultural life of the island, and trying them is a wonderful way to connect with local rhythms.

Above all, remember this: in Cyprus, food is never just food. It's family, history, nature, and love — served warm, meant to be shared, and always enjoyed with time on your side.

Cycling Routes and Mountain Biking

There's no better way to feel the rhythm of South Cyprus than by bike. Whether you're chasing coastal breezes, winding through mountain villages, or pushing up dirt trails through pine forests, cycling offers an intimate, exhilarating way to see the island. South Cyprus has quietly become a rising star for cycling tourism thanks to its excellent weather, diverse landscapes, and well-maintained road networks. With routes ranging from relaxing beachside rides to technical off-road mountain trails, this destination invites both beginners and experienced riders to explore its beauty on two wheels.

Unlike many destinations where cycling is just about sport, in Cyprus it's also about discovery. On a bike, you get close to the details — the smell of wild herbs by the roadside, the crunch of gravel under your tires, the quiet curve of a hilltop road, and the welcome sight of a village square café after a long climb. The pace may be yours to choose, but the reward is always the same: freedom and a fresh connection to the land.

Start your journey along the coast — it's the most accessible and visually stunning way to ease into cycling here. The **Limassol Coastal Route** is one of the most enjoyable rides in South Cyprus. This paved path stretches for several kilometers, hugging the seafront and passing through beach parks, archaeological sites, and lively cafés. It's a relaxed, flat ride that's perfect for beginners, families, or anyone just wanting to soak in the sea air and stop often for coffee or a dip in the water.

Further west, the **Paphos coastline** offers another beautiful route, especially the path from **Paphos Harbour to Coral Bay**. While not fully paved, this ride combines sea views with little detours into nature, and it's popular with casual riders. Sunset rides here are especially beautiful, as the light turns golden and the sea glows orange on the horizon.

For a more immersive cultural ride, the **Lefkara and Vavla villages route** is perfect. These rolling countryside roads lead you through sleepy stone villages, terraced hillsides, olive groves, and wineries. The terrain offers a mix of easy and moderate climbs, and you'll want to stop frequently — not just to catch your breath, but to explore local lace shops, taste homemade spoon sweets, and chat with the warm locals. This ride is less about speed and more about taking in the old-world charm of rural Cyprus.

For thrill-seekers and nature lovers, the **Troodos Mountains** are a cycling playground. Routes like **Platres to Mount Olympus** or **Kakopetria to Troodos Square** offer cooler temperatures, pine-scented forests, and a satisfying mix of road and mountain biking opportunities. The climb is real — but so are the views. From the ridges, you can often see down to both coasts of the island on a clear day. The Troodos range also has multiple dirt trails for serious mountain biking, ranging from loose gravel descents to technical forest single tracks.

Then there's **Akamas Peninsula**, a raw, untamed region ideal for confident mountain bikers. The terrain here is rocky, wild, and remote. Off-road tracks wind through gorges, climb rugged hills, and descend toward hidden beaches and isolated viewpoints. It's physically demanding but emotionally rewarding — especially when you stop for a break overlooking the Blue Lagoon or ride through ancient carob trees in total silence.

Cycling in South Cyprus is best during the cooler months — especially from **October to May** — when temperatures are pleasant and the landscape is green and blooming. While summer is still possible, it's best to ride early in the morning or late in the evening to avoid the intense midday heat. Always carry plenty of water, wear a hat or helmet, and apply sunscreen liberally, as the sun here can be intense even in spring and autumn.

There are **bike rental shops** in all major tourist hubs including Limassol, Paphos, Ayia Napa, Larnaca, and many villages in the Troodos region. Rental prices range from **€10 to €30 per day**, depending on the type of bike — with mountain bikes, road bikes, and e-bikes all available. Most rentals come with helmets, locks, and sometimes maps or route suggestions. Some also offer multi-day discounts, guided tours, or even delivery to your hotel.

For **serious cyclists**, bringing your own gear is not uncommon. If you're planning a full cycling holiday, there are also **cycling-friendly hotels** across the island that provide bike storage, repair areas, laundry service for gear, and hearty meals to refuel after long rides.

Traffic in Cyprus is relatively light on rural and mountain roads, but be cautious. Drivers are generally respectful, but road shoulders can be narrow or non-existent in places. Always wear bright clothing, especially if riding near dusk or dawn. Local laws require helmets for off-road cycling and recommend them for all riders.

Maps for popular cycling routes are available at tourist information offices and bike shops, and digital navigation apps like Komoot, Strava, or Ride with GPS are useful tools — particularly in more remote areas like Akamas where signs may be sparse. Mobile signal is generally good, but can drop in the most rugged parts of the island, so it's smart to download your route offline in advance.

For those who want to **ride but skip the planning**, several companies offer **cycling tours**, from half-day city routes to full-week cycling adventures through mountains and coast. These tours often include support vans, guides, meals, and accommodation, making it easy to just ride and enjoy.

Ultimately, whether you're pedaling past vineyards, climbing toward cloud-kissed peaks, or racing the wind along a stretch of empty beach road, cycling in South Cyprus offers something special. It's not just about the distance or the speed — it's about how the road makes you feel. And on this island, every road feels like it's leading somewhere worth discovering.

Rock Climbing and Caving

If you're the kind of traveler who seeks adventure carved in stone and hidden beneath the earth, South Cyprus offers a surprising and rewarding playground. While it's better known for its beaches and archaeological wonders, the island's rugged interior and wild coastlines are quietly becoming a favorite among rock climbers and caving enthusiasts. With limestone cliffs, gorges, sea caves, and quiet mountain walls, this island blends raw natural beauty with accessible, year-round climbing opportunities.

Here, climbing isn't about fame or record-breaking walls — it's about the joy of ascent in a place where the views are as rewarding as the routes. And beneath the surface, Cyprus also holds secrets: ancient sea caves carved by time, narrow passageways hidden in forested hills, and cool, echoing chambers that whisper of adventure. Whether you're a seasoned climber or a curious beginner, South Cyprus invites you to get vertical or go underground — safely, slowly, and always with wonder.

One of the most popular destinations for climbers is **Cape Greco**, located between Ayia Napa and Protaras. This headland offers striking sea cliffs, spectacular views, and a collection of limestone routes perfect for sport climbing. Though the walls here are not especially tall, the climbing is scenic, accessible, and wonderfully refreshing, thanks to the nearby ocean breeze. The terrain suits intermediate climbers, but beginners can also find easier routes or try their hand at bouldering near the cliffs. What makes Cape Greco unique is the combination of height and sea — you can literally climb above the sparkling turquoise waters, with the sound of waves crashing beneath you.

Further inland, the **Dhiarizos Valley** and the rocky areas near **Paphos and Episkopi** offer a different kind of climbing experience — quieter, more remote, and rich with natural formations. Limestone outcrops and shaded faces provide varied grades for different skill levels. These areas are less polished and more wild, often requiring a bit of hiking to access, but the reward is solitude and a connection to the raw landscape that's hard to find elsewhere. In these inland zones, it's not unusual to find yourself completely alone with the rock and the birdsong.

For bouldering and sport climbing in the mountains, **Troodos** delivers. The granite formations around **Platres**, **Moniatis**, and **Kakopetria** provide challenging terrain for technical climbers. While Troodos is more famous for hiking, those who venture with ropes and chalk bags will find steep, interesting faces with little crowding and cooler temperatures — a dream combination, especially in the hotter months.

When it comes to caving, South Cyprus doesn't have vast underground systems like other parts of Europe, but it does offer intriguing **sea caves and natural chambers**, many of which can be explored on foot or with simple gear. The **Sea Caves of Ayia Napa** and **Pegeia (near Coral Bay)** are especially dramatic. These caves have been shaped by thousands of years of waves carving into the coastline, forming arches, passageways, and echoing caverns that can be explored during low tide or calm sea conditions. Some can be entered by swimming or kayaking, while others are reachable by clambering down rocky ledges from above.

Another fascinating stop is the **Choirokoitia cave area**, located near the famous Neolithic site. Though not a commercial cave, it includes a small cluster of natural rock shelters used by early settlers and is worth a visit for those interested in combining history and exploration. Always proceed with caution, as these are unregulated sites, and while beautiful, they require basic outdoor awareness and appropriate footwear.

Climbing and caving in South Cyprus are best enjoyed during the **cooler months from October to May**. Summer can be extremely hot, especially on exposed rock faces or inside sea caves with little air movement. If you're planning to climb during summer, aim for early mornings or shaded areas, and always bring plenty of water and sun protection.

There are **no national regulations that restrict recreational rock climbing**, but climbers are expected to follow Leave No Trace principles, avoid damaging natural formations, and stay off archaeological sites or private land. Sea caves should be approached with caution — always check tide times, weather conditions, and sea swells before entering. During windy days, waves can flood cave entrances quickly and without warning.

Climbing gear can be rented from a few specialized **outdoor shops in Limassol and Nicosia**, and there are also **guided climbing experiences** available in Cape Greco, Troodos, and the Paphos area. These guided tours are highly recommended for beginners or anyone unfamiliar with the terrain. Prices typically range from **€40 to €80 per person**, including instruction, gear, and insurance. Group sizes are usually small, and many guides offer customized routes based on experience level.

For independent climbers, **guidebooks and route maps** are limited, though some local climbing communities maintain online forums and Facebook groups where you can get updated information, safety tips, and even coordinate with local climbers. It's also helpful to download offline maps and GPS data if you're heading to remote areas, as phone signal may be weak or nonexistent in the mountains and cliffs.

Good shoes are essential, even for sea caves — the rocks can be sharp and slippery, and protection is better than a bruised foot or worse. For caves and cliff areas, always wear a helmet, carry a flashlight or headlamp, and let someone know where you're going, especially if you're exploring alone.

Lastly, respect for the land is key. South Cyprus is a developing outdoor adventure destination, and part of what makes it special is how wild and unspoiled many of these locations remain. Don't mark the rock, leave behind trash, or damage the caves — and this natural playground will remain open for everyone to enjoy.

Skiing and Snowboarding on Mount Olympus

It may come as a surprise to many, but South Cyprus — known for its beaches and sun-soaked coastline — is also home to a ski destination where snow dusts the peaks and pine forests turn white in winter. Nestled in the heart of the **Troodos Mountains**, **Mount Olympus**, the highest point in Cyprus, offers a short but magical season for **skiing and snowboarding**, where you can carve through fresh powder by morning and relax at a seaside taverna by sunset. It's a unique and rare experience, and one of the few places in the world where you can go from the slopes to the sand in the same day.

The ski season in Cyprus is short and sweet — typically running from **late January through March** — but when the snow falls, the mountain transforms. The air turns crisp, the evergreens stand tall under a fresh blanket of snow, and the mood shifts from island-slow to alpine-ready. It's not a massive resort, but that's part of the charm. Skiing here feels personal, old-school, and utterly unexpected.

Mount Olympus reaches a height of **1,952 meters** and is home to the **Cyprus Ski Club**, which operates a small but active ski area on its northern face. There are four main slopes, each named after ancient Greek gods: **Aphrodite**, **Hermes**, **Hera**, and **Zeus**. These runs offer a mix of difficulty levels, making them suitable for both beginners and more experienced skiers or snowboarders looking for a fun day on the slopes rather than high-adrenaline challenges.

The **Hermes and Hera slopes** are gentle and great for first-timers or those brushing up on their technique. Meanwhile, **Zeus**, the longest and most advanced slope, offers a satisfying descent through pine-covered terrain. The **Aphrodite run** provides something in between, with a gentle but scenic glide perfect for intermediate riders or those simply looking to enjoy the view as they go.

The ski center offers **rental equipment**, **lessons**, and a **ski school**, making it accessible for visitors who didn't plan to ski when packing. There are **drag lifts** and **surface lifts** (no gondolas or chairlifts), which contribute to the retro, no-fuss atmosphere of the mountain. Crowds are generally small on weekdays, with weekends attracting more local families and hobbyists.

Snowboarders are welcome, and the slopes cater equally well to them, though there's no dedicated terrain park or freestyle features. Still, the natural surroundings, the peaceful trails, and the novelty of snowboarding in Cyprus make it a fun experience, especially when combined with a day trip or an overnight stay in one of the nearby villages.

Beyond the skiing itself, Mount Olympus and its surrounding area offer **snow-covered walking trails**, scenic viewpoints, and cozy mountain cafés serving hot drinks, homemade pastries, and traditional Cypriot comfort food — perfect for warming up after a few hours in the snow. The nearby villages of **Platres**, **Prodromos**, and **Troodos Square** offer a range of restaurants and lodges where you can unwind, refuel, and even stay the night for a full mountain escape.

The skiing season is short and heavily dependent on weather. Snow usually arrives in **January**, peaks in **February**, and starts to melt by the **end of March**. Conditions can vary from year to year, so it's important to check **local forecasts**, **Cyprus Ski Club updates**, and **webcams** before planning your visit. The ski area typically operates as long as there is adequate snow, but heavy storms or warm spells may temporarily interrupt the season.

The **Cyprus Ski Club**, located near Troodos Square, manages the slopes and provides ski passes, equipment rentals, and basic facilities. Rental prices for skis or snowboards, including boots and poles, usually range from **€20 to €30 per day**, and ski passes are relatively affordable, generally **€15 to €25 per day**, depending on age and number of lifts used. Discounts are often available for children and students.

Getting to Mount Olympus is easiest by car. The drive from **Limassol** takes about **one hour**, and from **Nicosia or Paphos**, it's roughly **90 minutes**. Roads are usually well-maintained but can be icy or snowy during the peak of winter, so driving with caution — and ideally with snow tires or chains — is highly advised. Parking is available near the slopes but fills up quickly on weekends or snow days.

There is **no on-mountain accommodation**, but nearby villages such as **Platres**, **Pedoulas**, and **Prodromos** offer mountain hotels, guesthouses, and traditional inns. These small towns are charming and make the whole experience feel like a cozy alpine retreat, complete with fireplaces, hearty mountain food, and clear night skies.

It's worth noting that Mount Olympus isn't a destination for professional skiers or serious alpine athletes, but for casual riders, families, and travelers seeking a unique winter experience in a warm-weather country, it's something quite special. The novelty of skiing in Cyprus, combined with the charm of the mountains and the chance to dip your toes in the sea later that day, creates memories that few destinations can match.

Horseback Riding

Few experiences feel as timeless and grounding as exploring the landscape on horseback. In South Cyprus, horseback riding is more than a leisurely outing — it's a chance to slow down, reconnect with nature, and experience the island from a completely different perspective. Whether you're trotting through pine-scented forests in the mountains, cantering along the coast with the sea breeze on your face, or riding at sunset beneath golden skies, Cyprus offers some unforgettable horseback moments for beginners and experienced riders alike.

The terrain across the island is ideal for riding — with hills, valleys, olive groves, vineyards, and panoramic views that stretch from the countryside to the sea. And thanks to the warm climate and mostly dry ground, horseback riding is available nearly all year round. What makes it even more special is the welcoming nature of local riding schools and ranches, where guests are treated like family, and the horses are not just well-trained — they're truly loved.

One of the most magical horseback experiences in South Cyprus is riding near the coast. Around **Paphos**, several riding centers offer scenic beachside and countryside trails. Picture yourself riding gently across open fields, through citrus orchards and small forests, eventually arriving at viewpoints where the Mediterranean glimmers in the distance. In some areas, sunset rides are a favorite, offering a soft orange glow over the hills and sea — a memory that stays long after the trip ends.

Near **Avdimou and Episkopi**, riding stables provide guided treks through the countryside with routes that pass by historic ruins, quiet village paths, and olive groves. It's not uncommon to spot herds of goats along the trail, or hear the call of birds in the trees above. These rides are slow-paced and tranquil, perfect for beginners or those who simply want to enjoy nature without a rush.

In the **Troodos region**, mountain riding is another kind of wonder altogether. Cool, crisp air replaces the coastal heat, and trails wind through dense pine forests, offering breathtaking views from the hills. Riding through these forests feels almost enchanted — with dappled sunlight falling through the trees, the rhythmic sound of hooves on forest paths, and the occasional encounter with local wildlife like hares or wild birds.

Ranches here offer a deeper dive into the riding experience. Many are family-owned and will walk you through the stables, introduce you to their horses by name, and match you with one based on your skill level and comfort. Some even allow hands-on grooming time before or after the ride, which adds a personal connection to the horse and creates a more meaningful experience.

For the more experienced rider, there are options for faster-paced rides and longer treks — some lasting up to half a day or more. These often include picnic breaks or stops at quiet viewpoints and are best booked in advance to ensure the route and pace are tailored to your abilities.

Horseback riding is available all year round in Cyprus, with the most comfortable seasons being **spring and autumn** when the weather is mild and the landscapes are lush. During **summer**, riding is still possible but typically scheduled early in the morning or around sunset to avoid the midday heat. In **winter**, rides in the lower altitudes continue comfortably, while mountain routes offer a refreshing, misty experience.

There are several reputable riding centers across the island, particularly near **Paphos, Limassol, Troodos**, and **Larnaca**. Most accept walk-ins, but booking ahead is always recommended, especially for sunset rides or weekend slots. Rides typically range in duration from **30 minutes to 2 hours**, with prices starting around **€25 to €30 for a short ride**, and going up to **€50 to €70** for longer or private sessions. Packages for families or couples are often available, and some ranches also offer special rides for children, complete with lessons and pony grooming sessions.

Most stables provide helmets and all necessary safety equipment. Beginners are warmly welcomed, and rides are guided at all times, with instructors making sure each rider is comfortable before setting off. The horses are usually calm, well-trained, and used to carrying inexperienced riders, making the experience both enjoyable and safe.

Wear **closed shoes**, preferably boots or sturdy sneakers, and **long pants** to protect your legs from rubbing against the saddle. Sunscreen, water, and a light jacket (for mountain rides) are recommended depending on the season. Photography is welcomed during the ride, and many guides are happy to snap a picture or two for you at scenic stops.

It's worth noting that Cyprus takes animal care seriously, and most of the riding schools emphasize the well-being of their horses. If in doubt, a quick visit to the stable before booking can reassure you about the conditions and care. A good sign is horses that look healthy, are well-fed, and are treated with patience and affection by their handlers.

Above all, horseback riding in South Cyprus is not just an activity — it's an experience that invites you to slow your pace, breathe deeply, and appreciate the island's natural beauty in a way few other adventures can. Whether it's your first time in a saddle or your hundredth, the trails of Cyprus are waiting.

Paragliding and Aerial Tours

There's something profoundly humbling — and incredibly thrilling — about seeing South Cyprus from the sky. Floating high above the coast, watching golden beaches curve into turquoise water, and gazing across mountain peaks that fall away into patchwork valleys below, is an experience that few forget. Paragliding and aerial tours in Cyprus offer a whole new perspective on the island: one that blends the adrenaline of flight with the quiet awe of nature in its grandest form.

Whether you're soaring silently on the wind during a tandem paragliding flight or zipping across the island in a light aircraft or helicopter, these experiences tap into the spirit of freedom and adventure. For those who dare to rise above it all, Cyprus doesn't just impress — it stuns.

One of the most popular spots for **paragliding** in South Cyprus is near the town of **Droushia**, in the **Paphos region**. Here, the cliffs and thermal currents create perfect conditions for long, graceful flights. Tandem paragliding is the most common option — no experience is needed, and you're securely strapped to an experienced pilot who handles the launch, flight, and landing. You simply take a few steps off a gentle slope and before you know it, you're gliding smoothly through the air with panoramic views stretching across the **Akamas Peninsula**, **Lara Bay**, and out to the sea. It's peaceful, surreal, and often described as the closest thing to flying like a bird.

Another exceptional location is **Konia**, also near Paphos, where the takeoff sites are higher, giving you longer flights and more dramatic aerial views. Depending on weather and wind conditions, flights can last anywhere from **15 to 30 minutes**, with altitude often reaching over **800 meters**. The landscape below shifts between rugged coastline, sprawling vineyards, sleepy villages, and craggy ridges — every glance a postcard.

For those who prefer a more structured and extensive view from above, **aerial tours** in light planes or helicopters are also available. These tours offer a more controlled and wide-reaching experience, often departing from small airfields near **Larnaca** or **Paphos**, and flying over key sights like **Cape Greco**, the **Salt Lakes**, the **Troodos Mountains**, and ancient ruins like **Kourion**. On a clear day, you can sometimes see across to the northern parts of the island — a rare and beautiful bonus.

Helicopter rides add a touch of luxury and flexibility. Some companies even offer private flights with custom routes, making it a romantic option for couples or a bucket-list treat for adventure seekers. These flights are smooth and come with guided commentary through headsets, so you get to enjoy both the view and the story behind what you're seeing.

Paragliding is available year-round, but the **best flying conditions are from March to November**, when thermals are stable, skies are clear, and wind patterns are ideal. Flights may be rescheduled due to sudden weather changes, so it's recommended to book a flexible time or keep a day open just in case. Most tandem paragliding sessions include a short briefing, safety gear, and an optional GoPro video or photo package for an additional fee.

No prior experience is needed to paraglide — just a sense of adventure and a willingness to trust your pilot. Wear comfortable clothes and sturdy shoes (no sandals or flip-flops), and be sure to bring sunglasses. Motion sickness is rare, but if you're sensitive to altitude or nerves, light snacks and hydration beforehand are helpful.

Paragliding sessions usually cost between **€80 to €120 per person**, depending on location, flight time, and any extras like in-flight photography. All equipment is provided, and pilots are certified and highly trained. Insurance is typically included in the cost, but always double-check when booking.

Aerial tours by plane or helicopter generally start around **€150 to €300** per person, with private flights costing more depending on the route and duration. Flights can last from **20 minutes to over an hour**, and the operators provide headsets, safety briefings, and commentary during the ride. Booking in advance is essential, especially during the high season, and passports or ID may be required at some small airfields due to flight regulations.

Safety standards are high, and flight operators are licensed and regulated. However, as with any aviation activity, there are strict weather-related restrictions, so being flexible with your timing is crucial. If you're booking a flight as part of a special occasion — like a honeymoon or birthday — mention it in advance, as many operators are happy to offer small surprises or perks to make the moment even more memorable.

These sky-high experiences in South Cyprus add a layer of magic to your journey. They allow you to grasp the scale and natural beauty of the island in a way no map or photo ever could. From the soft lift-off of a paraglider to the thrilling hover of a helicopter, you'll leave the ground — and take a little piece of Cyprus with you, forever etched in memory.

HIDDEN GEMS AND OFF-THE-BEATEN-PATH

Lefkara Village (Lace and Silver)

When you step into Lefkara, it doesn't feel like just another village — it feels like time has taken a slower pace here. The streets are narrow and quiet, paved with stone and lined with charming old houses, each with wooden shutters and bougainvillea climbing up the walls. You'll hear the faint clinking of tools as local silversmiths work, and the soft, rhythmic motion of lace being hand-stitched by women sitting in shaded corners. This village isn't just a place to visit — it's a story to walk through, a piece of Cyprus that has held tightly to its traditions while the rest of the world has rushed ahead.

As you explore, you'll quickly notice that Lefkara is famous for two things: its **lace** and its **silverwork**. These crafts are not just souvenirs — they're living art. The lace, known as "Lefkaritika," is delicate and detailed, passed down through generations. It's said that even Leonardo da Vinci took a piece back to Italy when he visited centuries ago. You'll see it displayed proudly in shop windows, spread across tables, and being made right in front of you by women who learned from their mothers and grandmothers.

And then there's the silver. Handmade filigree jewelry, old-fashioned tools, tiny boxes, and elegant crosses — all crafted with patience and skill. Many shops double as workshops, and if you're curious, don't hesitate to peek inside and ask questions. The silversmiths are often happy to show you how the process works, explaining as they go. It's a great way to connect to the heart of the village, not just as a tourist, but as a guest in someone's story.

But Lefkara isn't just about crafts. It has a calm energy that invites you to slow down. Maybe you'll stop for a coffee at a local café where old men are playing backgammon. Or maybe you'll follow the winding alleys uphill to find a small church with stunning frescoes, or pause to take in the mountain views that open up when you least expect them. Every corner of this village offers something — a mural, a potted plant, a cat asleep on a windowsill — that reminds you life doesn't need to be hurried to be beautiful.

If you're hungry, you're in luck. The food in Lefkara is simple, hearty, and made with love. You'll find traditional tavernas serving dishes like sheftalia, halloumi, and slow-cooked meats, often with a glass of village wine that pairs perfectly with the relaxed pace of your afternoon. Many restaurants here use ingredients from the area, and you can taste the difference.

You don't need a checklist or a tight schedule in Lefkara. The best thing to do is wander. Let yourself get a little lost in the quiet streets. Take your time visiting a lace shop, then sit down and let a local tell you a story or two. You'll learn more about the village that way than any signpost could ever explain.

Lefkara is located in the **Larnaca District**, about a **40-minute drive from Larnaca city**, and just over an hour from **Nicosia** or **Limassol**. It's best reached by car, though some tours include it as part of a cultural route. The village itself is free to visit, and there's no need for tickets or entrance fees unless you're stepping into a small museum or gallery — most of which ask for a few euros at most. The **Museum of Traditional Embroidery and Silversmithing**, located right in the village, is worth a visit if you're curious about how these crafts have survived and evolved.

Shops typically open from **9:00 AM to 6:00 PM**, though smaller family-run places might close for a break in the early afternoon, especially during summer. Sundays are quieter, but not completely closed down, and you'll still find some cafés and souvenir spots open.

You don't come to Lefkara for big thrills or long lines. You come here to see a different side of Cyprus — one that's slow, sincere, and deeply proud of its heritage. It's a reminder that sometimes the most beautiful places aren't hidden at all. They're just quiet enough to be missed if you're not paying attention.

Agios Nikolaos tis Stegis Church

If you ever feel like stepping off the main road and slipping into the past, then make your way to the Agios Nikolaos tis Stegis Church. Tucked away in the mountains near **Kakopetria village**, this small, quiet church might not grab your attention from the outside — but once you step inside, it tells a story that's over a thousand years old. This isn't just a place of worship. It's a piece of Cyprus that has stood quietly for centuries, filled with secrets painted on its walls.

The name means "Saint Nicholas of the Roof," and once you see it, the name makes perfect sense. Unlike other churches in Cyprus, this one is covered with a steep, wooden roof — built to protect it from the rain and snow that fall in the Troodos Mountains. It looks more like a countryside barn than a church from the outside. But the moment you walk in, you're surrounded by something entirely different — ancient, colorful frescoes that cover nearly every inch of the walls and ceilings.

Inside, it feels peaceful. The light is dim, filtered through small windows, and there's a coolness in the air that makes you slow down. You'll see painted scenes of saints, angels, and biblical stories — some faded with time, others still incredibly vivid. The artwork spans centuries, with pieces dating back to the **11th century**, making this church one of the finest examples of **Byzantine art** in Cyprus. What's special about it isn't just the art itself, but the way it has been preserved, quietly and without fanfare, in this mountain setting.

As you look around, you might notice details you don't usually see in larger, more polished churches — a hand reaching out from a wall, the worn faces of saints, tiny details painted with care in corners where few might even look. This place invites you to pay attention. It's not flashy. It's real.

While you're here, take your time. Let yourself sit down in the stillness and take it all in. There's something humbling about being in a place that has stood for so long, in silence, watching the world change all around it. And when you leave, the surrounding landscape offers its own kind of beauty — quiet hills, pine trees, and the gentle hum of wind through the mountains.

You'll find the church just outside the village of **Kakopetria**, about **two kilometers to the south**, in the **Troodos region**. It's about an **hour and a half drive from Nicosia**, and just under **two hours from Limassol**. Getting there is easiest by car, and the road winds through scenic countryside that's worth the drive in itself.

There is **no entrance fee**, but it's always appreciated to leave a small donation to support the church's maintenance. The church is usually open **Tuesday to Saturday from 9:00 AM to 4:00 PM**, and **Sundays from 11:00 AM to 4:00 PM**. It's closed on Mondays. However, opening times can vary slightly depending on the season, so it's a good idea to visit earlier in the day to avoid missing out.

Photography is not always allowed inside, especially with flash, as it can damage the centuries-old frescoes. It's best to ask the caretaker or guide on duty. If you're lucky, someone will be there to explain a bit more about the history — often not a professional tour guide, but a local who knows the stories well and shares them with quiet pride.

This church is part of the **UNESCO World Heritage list** of painted churches in the Troodos region, though it rarely gets the attention or crowds that other tourist landmarks receive. That's exactly why it feels so special. It's the kind of place that reminds you how rich Cyprus is in hidden beauty, and how sometimes the quietest places leave the loudest impression.

Saint Hilarion Castle

You don't just visit Saint Hilarion Castle — you climb into a fairy tale. Perched high in the mountains above **Kyrenia**, this castle doesn't feel like it belongs in the real world. With its towers poking through the clouds and sweeping views that stretch all the way to the coast, it feels more like a fantasy movie set than a historical ruin. But it's real. And the moment you step onto its weathered stone path, you can almost hear the echoes of knights' boots and royal whispers carried on the wind.

As you begin your walk up the mountain, the castle reveals itself bit by bit. There's a lower section, a middle courtyard, and a final stretch that leads to the top — each one offering a new reward if you're willing to climb just a little further. Don't rush. This isn't just a quick photo stop. This is a place to wander, to explore slowly, and to let your imagination roam as freely as the goats you might see climbing the cliffs nearby.

The castle itself dates back to the **10th century**, originally built as a monastery before it became a fortress and summer retreat for the Lusignan kings. You'll pass through arched gates and winding staircases, with parts of the structure still surprisingly well-preserved. Some rooms still have windows with stone seats, once used by guards or royals to look out over the valleys below. There are hidden chambers, long-forgotten stairways, and lookout points that offer jaw-dropping views over the island and out to sea.

Legend has it that Saint Hilarion Castle inspired the castle in Disney's *Snow White*. It's easy to believe when you're standing on a turret, looking down over the layered rooftops of what once was a royal residence nestled into the cliffs. The middle section has what's believed to be the queen's quarters — and whether or not the stories are all true, it adds to the feeling that magic still lingers in the air up here.

But even without the legends, it's the view that stays with you. From the top, the landscape rolls out in every direction — the **Kyrenia coastline**, the **Mediterranean Sea**, and even the **northern plains** of the island. On a clear day, you might even catch a faint outline of the Turkish coast in the distance. It's the kind of view that reminds you just how much history this place has seen, and how lucky you are to be standing in the middle of it.

Getting to Saint Hilarion Castle takes a bit of effort, but it's worth every step. The castle is located in **Northern Cyprus**, just above **Kyrenia (Girne)**, and you'll need a car or a tour to reach it. The drive itself is scenic, winding through the **Kyrenia mountain range**. Once you arrive, there's a parking area at the base, and from there, you'll follow a steep path with stairs and stone walkways up through the ruins. It's a bit of a hike, so wear comfortable shoes, and bring water — especially in the warmer months.

The castle is open **daily from around 9:00 AM to 5:00 PM**, though hours can change slightly depending on the season. Entrance costs **around €2 to €3** (or the local equivalent), making it one of the best-value experiences in the region. There's often a small ticket booth at the entrance, and while facilities are limited, you'll find restrooms and sometimes a small café or vendor near the parking area.

Because the castle is in **Northern Cyprus**, you'll need to cross the Green Line from the south if you're staying in places like Limassol, Larnaca, or Nicosia. The **border crossings are easy** with a valid passport, and many travelers make a day trip out of it. The blend of landscapes and cultures between the two sides of the island makes the journey even more interesting.

There aren't many signs or ropes blocking areas inside the castle, so you're free to explore at your own pace — just be cautious on uneven steps and high edges. It's a real castle ruin, which means no polished handrails or safety barriers, but that's exactly what makes it feel so raw and authentic.

When you walk back down after exploring the top, you'll probably feel a bit tired — but more than that, you'll feel like you just uncovered one of Cyprus's best-kept secrets. Saint Hilarion isn't as crowded as the big-name ruins or tourist hotspots, and that's part of its charm. It's wild, dramatic, and unforgettable — the kind of place that makes you feel like you've discovered something special before the rest of the world catches on.

Avakas Gorge

If you're someone who loves getting a little muddy, hearing nothing but the sound of your footsteps and rushing water, and finding yourself completely surrounded by nature — then you're going to fall in love with Avakas Gorge. This place isn't about polished trails or big signs pointing you where to go. It's raw, wild, and absolutely breathtaking — one of those hidden treasures that makes you feel like you've wandered straight into a nature documentary.

The gorge lies in the **Akamas Peninsula**, not far from **Paphos**, but once you're inside, you feel a world away from the beaches and the buzz. The hike takes you deep between towering limestone walls that rise over your head — sometimes more than **30 meters high**. These walls curve and twist, shaped over thousands of years by the small stream that still flows at your feet. In places, the passage narrows so much that you can stretch out your arms and touch both sides at once.

The deeper you go, the quieter it gets. You'll hear the crunch of your steps on gravel, the drip of water from the mossy walls, and the occasional call of a bird echoing overhead. It feels secret — like nature's own private corridor. In spring, the gorge is filled with wildflowers, butterflies, and bright green moss that adds color to the grey rock. In cooler months, you might see the stream flowing a bit faster, or catch sight of wild goats climbing impossibly steep cliff faces.

This hike isn't just a walk — it's an adventure. You'll cross the stream a few times, hop over stones, and duck under rocky arches. Some parts might be slippery or uneven, so it's not a place for flip-flops or rushed visits. But that's the beauty of it. You move slowly here, and every turn brings something new — a burst of sunlight cutting through the gap above, a tree growing sideways from the rock, or a quiet pool of water so still it looks like glass.

There's no "perfect" endpoint unless you're doing the full hike, which can take **1.5 to 2 hours each way**, depending on how far you want to go. Some travelers turn back after reaching the narrowest point — a natural stone arch deep inside — while others continue all the way until the path opens into fields on the other side. Either way, the journey is the reward here, not just the destination.

Avakas Gorge is located about **30 to 40 minutes from Paphos by car**, and the final part of the drive is on a dirt road. It's manageable, but a car with decent clearance helps. There's a small parking area at the trailhead, and from there, you'll start your walk into the gorge. There are no facilities — no shops, no toilets, no signs — so come prepared. Bring water, wear good shoes, and dress for the season. In summer, go early to avoid the heat, and in winter, be ready for mud and water crossings.

There is **no entrance fee**, and the gorge is open to the public year-round. That said, during or after heavy rains, parts of the trail can become slippery or even unsafe due to rising water. Locals will often know the conditions, so if you're unsure, it's worth asking around before heading out.

Avakas isn't the kind of place that's packed with tourists or tour buses. It's quiet, unspoiled, and easy to miss — which is exactly why it's such a gem. When you're standing in the middle of it, surrounded by stone, water, and sky, it's hard to believe that something this epic can exist without entry gates or long lines. It's just there, waiting for you to find it — and once you do, you'll carry it with you long after you've left.

Linos tou Charilaou Wine Press

You might think you know what a wine press looks like — maybe something modern, something stainless steel, something clean and mechanical. But when you step into **Linos tou Charilaou**, all of that disappears. What you find here is something much older, something handcrafted, and something that brings you face to face with Cyprus's deep-rooted wine-making heritage. This is not just a stop for wine lovers — it's a stop for anyone who wants to feel what it's like to touch history with their hands.

Tucked away in the sleepy village of **Omodos**, Linos tou Charilaou feels like you're walking into a quiet memory. The moment you pass through the wooden door, it's as if the modern world fades out. Inside, you're met with the sight of a huge traditional wine press made from massive beams of wood and stone — the kind that was used by hand and foot, where families worked together to turn grapes into something rich and full of life. The smell of old oak lingers in the air, mixed with the faint sweetness of dried grape skins and time.

This old winery, or "linos," belonged to the **Charilaou family**, and it has been beautifully preserved as a window into the past. You'll see the original tools used to crush and store the grapes, the wooden vats, and clay jars once used to hold the precious liquid. There's something honest about it all — no frills, no gloss, just the craft as it once was. It's easy to imagine the stories, the music, the laughter, and the effort that once filled this space during harvest season.

You're not just looking at things here — you're stepping into a way of life that shaped the village itself. In Cyprus, wine isn't just a drink. It's part of the culture, part of the table, and part of every gathering. And Linos tou Charilaou lets you see where that all began, long before bottled labels and gift shops.

As you explore the rest of **Omodos**, you'll notice how closely tied the village is to wine. There are local wineries nearby where you can taste different varieties, including the sweet **Commandaria** — one of the world's oldest named wines, still made using ancient methods. After stepping out of the wine press, it makes tasting the wine even more special. Now you know the story behind it.

Linos tou Charilaou is located right in the **heart of Omodos**, about **40 minutes from Limassol** by car, and just over an hour from Paphos or Nicosia. The village itself is lovely, full of stone buildings, cobbled streets, and family-run shops that sell lace, wine, and traditional sweets. It's one of those places where time seems to have slowed down, and every doorway leads to something unexpected.

Visiting the wine press is free, and it's open most days during daylight hours. Since it's part of the cultural walk through the village, you don't need a special ticket — you can just step inside and explore. During festivals or local celebrations, the space sometimes comes alive again with music, dancing, and storytelling, just as it might have been a hundred years ago.

If you enjoy discovering places that aren't packed with tourists but offer a genuine glimpse into a country's soul, then Linos tou Charilaou will be one of those spots that stays with you. It's not grand or flashy, but it's real — and sometimes, that's more powerful than anything else.

DAY TRIPS AND EXCURSIONS

Day Trip to the Akamas Peninsula

If you're craving a break from city life or crowded beaches, a day trip to the **Akamas Peninsula** is exactly what you need. This is where you trade pavement for dusty trails, noise for bird songs, and traffic for the sound of waves crashing against untouched coastline. The Akamas region, sitting quietly in the northwest corner of Cyprus, is wild, rugged, and absolutely unforgettable.

The minute you arrive, it's clear that this place has stayed mostly untouched — no massive resorts, no high-rise buildings, just nature as it's meant to be. The peninsula is protected for good reason. It's home to rare plants, endangered wildlife, dramatic landscapes, and ancient legends. And the best part is, you get to explore it your way. Whether you're into hiking, swimming, off-roading, or just sitting still in a place that feels completely unspoiled, the Akamas Peninsula has something for you.

One of the most popular spots to start your adventure is **Lara Bay**, famous as a nesting site for sea turtles. If you're lucky, and you visit during the right season, you might even catch a glimpse of tiny hatchlings making their first steps toward the sea. Even if not, the beach itself is stunning — wild and golden, with not much more than soft sand and clear water stretching for miles.

Further along, the **Baths of Aphrodite** offer a mix of mythology and beauty. According to legend, this is where the goddess of love used to bathe, hidden away in a quiet pool surrounded by fig trees and vines. Whether or not the story is true, the spot has a peaceful energy that makes you want to pause, take a deep breath, and just enjoy the stillness.

If you're up for a bit of movement, the **Aphrodite and Adonis nature trails** are two of the best ways to see the peninsula on foot. These marked paths take you up into the hills, where panoramic views of the sea and cliffs make every step worth it. Depending on your pace and route, you'll pass pine forests, rare plants, and lookout points that make for perfect photo stops. It's not a flat walk, so wear good shoes and bring water, but the sense of peace and the views are totally worth the effort.

Feeling adventurous? You can also explore Akamas by **jeep safari**, which is ideal if you want to cover more ground. These off-road tours bounce you through valleys, gorges, and remote beaches where few people go. Local guides often share stories, folklore, and a bit of humor along the way, turning a bumpy ride into a memorable journey.

You can reach the Akamas Peninsula easily from **Paphos**, which is about **a 45-minute drive** away. Most visitors enter from the **Latchi** side, where you can park and either hike, join a tour, or rent a buggy or quad bike to explore on your own. Some also choose to explore by sea, with boat trips from **Latchi Harbour** that cruise along the coastline and stop for swimming in spots like the **Blue Lagoon** — one of the clearest and most beautiful swimming spots in all of Cyprus.

There's **no entrance fee** to the peninsula itself, and you can explore freely from sunrise to sunset. However, if you book a guided tour or a jeep safari, prices usually range from **€25 to €60 per person**, depending on the length and inclusions. Boat trips can also vary in price, often including lunch or snorkeling gear.

Because it's a protected area, facilities are limited. There are no restaurants or big tourist shops inside the peninsula, so it's best to pack your own food, water, and anything else you might need for the day. There are small cafés and tavernas in **Latchi**, where you can grab a meal before or after your adventure.

What makes a day trip to Akamas so special isn't just the views or the activities — it's the feeling of freedom. You're not walking through a museum. You're walking through living, breathing nature. No crowds, no rush, just space to explore, disconnect, and reconnect with the beauty of the land. It's the kind of place you remember not because of a single photo, but because of how it made you feel.

Exploring the Karpas Peninsula

When you're ready to really escape — not just from your hotel, but from the tourist trails altogether — the **Karpas Peninsula** is where you go. This is the wild, untamed finger of land stretching off the northeastern tip of Cyprus, and it's unlike anywhere else on the island. Out here, the pace of life slows to a gentle rhythm, the beaches stretch on without end, and tiny villages feel as though time passed them by decades ago.

Exploring the Karpas feels like opening a secret chapter in the story of Cyprus. The further you drive in, the quieter it gets. The roads get narrower, the hills steeper, and the views wider. You'll pass through olive groves, fields of golden wheat, and sleepy stone-built villages where life is simple and genuine. This is where locals still wave at strangers, and the only sounds you hear might be a tractor in the distance or the breeze through carob trees.

One of the first stops that captures your attention is the **Apostolos Andreas Monastery**, standing proudly near the tip of the peninsula. It's an important pilgrimage site, especially for Greek Cypriots, and it carries a deep spiritual presence even for non-religious visitors. Set against a backdrop of cliffs and sea, it feels both peaceful and powerful. Inside, you'll find candles, icons, and quiet corners to pause and reflect. The location itself — right by the water — adds to its magic.

But the true treasure of the Karpas isn't just the buildings. It's the land. It's the freedom of standing on a beach where you might be the only person in sight. Take **Golden Beach**, for example. This stretch of soft sand and turquoise water is one of the most beautiful — and least crowded — on the entire island. You can lay your towel down, walk along the dunes, or swim in the crystal-clear sea without hearing a single car or seeing rows of umbrellas. It's nature at its purest.

Keep an eye out for the famous **Karpas wild donkeys** that roam freely across the peninsula. You'll probably meet a few along the road — they're friendly, curious, and often come right up to the car. It's one of those unexpected moments that makes the journey even more memorable.

If you're exploring by car, it's best to leave early in the morning and plan for a full-day adventure. The drive from **Nicosia** or **Famagusta** can take a few hours, and you'll want to stop often — not just for the sights, but because the road itself winds through some of the most scenic parts of northern Cyprus. Bring snacks, water, and maybe even a picnic, since places to eat are few and far between once you're deep in the peninsula. That said, if you do find a local taverna in one of the villages, it's almost guaranteed to be delicious and cooked with love.

There's no entrance fee to visit the Karpas or its major landmarks. The area is always open, and since it's not heavily commercialized, you're free to explore at your own pace. If you're visiting the monastery, donations are welcome, and modest clothing is appreciated as a sign of respect.

Because the Karpas is in **Northern Cyprus**, you'll need to cross the border if you're coming from the south. The process is simple — just bring your passport, and you can cross easily at several checkpoints. Renting a car that's insured for both sides of the island is the best way to go, especially if you want the flexibility to stop wherever you like.

What makes the Karpas Peninsula truly special is its untouched feeling. You don't come here for a list of attractions. You come here for the silence, the space, and the sense that you've found a part of the island that still belongs to itself. It's a reminder that the best parts of travel are often the ones without ticket lines, guided tours, or hashtags. Just you, the road, and the world as it once was.

Visit to the Troodos Mountains

When you need a break from the beach and crave fresh mountain air, cooler temperatures, and a different side of Cyprus altogether, heading into the **Troodos Mountains** is one of the best day trips you can take. Whether you're visiting in the heat of summer or the chill of winter, there's always something special waiting for you up here — hidden villages, forested trails, waterfalls, and quiet corners of the island that feel worlds away from the coastline.

As you wind your way up into the mountains, the scenery begins to change. Pine trees line the roads, the temperature drops, and the views stretch out over valleys and distant ridges. It's a welcome shift — a reminder that Cyprus isn't just about sunny beaches. Up here, nature takes over, and the pace of life slows down in the best possible way.

You'll want to make your way to the **Troodos Square**, which sits at the heart of the range and serves as a starting point for many adventures. From here, you can visit the majestic **Mount Olympus**, the highest peak in Cyprus, standing at nearly 2,000 meters. In the winter months, the mountain is often dusted with snow, and you might even find people skiing or snowboarding on its small but charming slopes. In summer, it's all about hiking and soaking up the peaceful atmosphere.

Beyond the views, one of the most rewarding parts of visiting the Troodos Mountains is exploring the **villages tucked into the hillsides**. Places like **Kakopetria**, **Platres**, and **Pedoulas** are not only beautiful but full of personality. Stone houses with red-tiled roofs, narrow alleys, and small family-run taverns make these spots perfect for wandering and grabbing a homemade meal. You'll often stumble across local shops selling mountain honey, handmade sweets, and traditional products you won't find anywhere else on the island.

If you love a bit of culture with your nature, don't miss the **painted churches of the Troodos region**. These UNESCO World Heritage sites are scattered across the mountains, and while they might look simple from the outside, the interiors are breathtaking. Frescoes dating back to the 11th and 12th centuries cover the walls and ceilings, telling stories through color and detail that have lasted through centuries. Even if you're not religious, the quiet beauty inside these chapels is something you won't forget.

The **Caledonia and Millomeris Waterfalls** are also highlights you can visit during your day trip. You'll need to take a short hike through shaded forest paths, but when you reach the falls, the sound of cascading water and the cool mist make it feel like a little paradise hidden away in the hills.

Getting to the Troodos Mountains from **Limassol**, **Nicosia**, or **Paphos** is easy by car and takes about **an hour to an hour and a half**, depending on your route. The roads are well-paved and offer some of the most scenic drives on the island. Parking is usually available in the villages and squares, and many of the trails and attractions are clearly marked, though it's always a good idea to bring a map or use GPS.

There are **no major entrance fees** for the mountains themselves, and visiting the villages, nature trails, and churches is often free. A few sites may ask for a small donation or a ticket under **€2 to €3**, especially the UNESCO churches or museums. The best time to visit is during spring or autumn, when the weather is mild and the forests are full of color, but summer offers an escape from the coastal heat, and winter has its own snowy charm.

Whether you come for a peaceful hike, a cozy lunch in a mountain taverna, or just a scenic drive through thick pine forests, the **Troodos Mountains** offer something that touches every kind of traveler. It's not flashy or fast-paced, but that's exactly what makes it beautiful. Up here, you're invited to slow down, breathe deep, and see a completely different side of Cyprus — one that's just as rich and rewarding as anything along the shore.

Cultural Tour of Lefkara and Omodos

If you're the kind of traveler who enjoys slow moments, rich traditions, and the quiet charm of village life, then spending a day in **Lefkara and Omodos** is going to be one of the most rewarding parts of your trip. These two villages may be small on the map, but they're bursting with history, artistry, and culture that you'll feel the moment you set foot on their cobbled streets.

Start your day with **Lefkara**, a village perched on the hillsides of the Larnaca district. This place is world-famous for one beautiful reason: **lace**. Known as *Lefkaritika*, the lacework here is so intricate and detailed that it once caught the eye of Leonardo da Vinci himself. The story goes that he visited the village and took a lace altar cloth back to Italy for the Duomo of Milan — and whether that's myth or fact, it gives you an idea of just how far this village's reputation has traveled.

As you stroll through the narrow streets, you'll see older women sitting in front of their homes, carefully stitching lace by hand — the same way it's been done for generations. Shops display delicate patterns that look like they belong in museums, yet they're made here, right in front of you. There's also a strong tradition of **silversmithing**, with family-run workshops selling handcrafted jewelry and ornaments that shimmer in the sunlight.

Take your time walking through **traditional stone houses**, visiting the **Lefkara Handicraft Centre**, and stopping by the **Folk Art Museum**, where you can learn more about the local way of life. There's something grounding about seeing the tools and objects of everyday life from centuries ago — simple, yet full of meaning.

After soaking up the charm of Lefkara, make your way to **Omodos**, a village in the **Limassol** district that's equally rich in culture, but with its own personality. Omodos is famous for its

wine, and even if you're not a wine expert, this is the perfect place to try a glass (or two) of local varieties — especially **Commandaria**, the sweet dessert wine that Cyprus has been producing for over 2,000 years.

Omodos is also home to the **Monastery of the Holy Cross**, a peaceful and sacred spot in the center of the village. Step inside to find quiet courtyards, ancient icons, and a sense of calm that contrasts beautifully with the lively buzz just outside. Around the monastery square, you'll find small cafes, family-run taverns, and artisan shops selling lace, sweets, and handmade goods. Grab a traditional Cypriot lunch here — maybe grilled halloumi, souvlaki, or moussaka — and enjoy it slowly, like the locals do.

One of the best parts about both villages is how relaxed everything feels. There's no rush, no long lines, and no crowds pushing past you. It's the kind of day where you're allowed to wander aimlessly, sip coffee under a shady vine, and strike up conversations with shopkeepers who are happy to share a story or two.

Getting to **Lefkara** takes about **40 minutes from Larnaca** or just over **an hour from Nicosia**. From there, you can continue on to **Omodos**, which is another **hour's drive**, making it an ideal full-day loop through two of Cyprus's most culturally rich villages. The roads are scenic, winding through mountains and hills, and you'll want to pull over for photos more than once.

There are **no entrance fees** to explore either village, though small museums or workshops might ask for a couple of euros if you want a closer look. Most shops, cafes, and attractions are open from **morning until early evening**, though like much of the island, things tend to move at a relaxed pace — so it's best to avoid rushing and enjoy whatever the day brings.

A cultural tour through Lefkara and Omodos is less about ticking off attractions and more about soaking in a way of life. It's for travelers who love discovering the stories behind the places they visit, who enjoy the slow beauty of craftsmanship, and who find joy in the little moments — the ones that stay with you long after the trip ends.

Coastal Boat Tours and Cruises

Sometimes, the best way to see Cyprus isn't by road — it's from the water. When you step onto a boat and drift away from the shore, something shifts. The crowds disappear, the breeze picks up, and suddenly you're looking back at the coastline in a way you've never seen before. A **coastal boat tour or cruise** isn't just a relaxing activity — it's an entirely different perspective on the island, full of hidden coves, sea caves, and crystal-clear swimming spots you'd never reach on foot.

You'll find boat tours offered in several coastal towns, but some of the most popular and scenic ones leave from **Ayia Napa**, **Protaras**, **Paphos**, and **Latchi**. Each of these places offers a slightly different experience, depending on what kind of vibe you're after. Some cruises are laid-back and quiet, perfect for couples or solo travelers who just want to float in peace, while others are lively and social, with music, food, and a bit of dancing on deck.

If you're setting off from **Ayia Napa or Protaras**, expect dramatic cliffs, rock arches, and some of the bluest water you've ever seen. One of the highlights here is the **Sea Caves** — hollowed out by the waves and perfect for photos. Many boats anchor nearby so you can jump into the water or snorkel around. Further along, you'll see the **Blue Lagoon**, where the water is so clear it looks like it belongs in a postcard. The swimming here is unbeatable.

In **Paphos**, cruises often follow a different coastline, with a mix of historical landmarks and quieter waters. Some tours include views of ancient shipwrecks, while others drift past lighthouses and rocky outcrops that make the coastline feel rugged and wild. If you're lucky, you might even spot sea turtles or dolphins playing in the surf.

From **Latchi**, the experience feels a little more untouched. This is the starting point for boat trips to the **Akamas Peninsula**, one of the most protected and naturally beautiful parts of the island. Out here, you'll feel like you've left civilization behind. The boats often stop at the **Blue Lagoon of Akamas**, and you'll have time to swim, snorkel, or just float under the sun. Some tours also include a stop near the **Baths of Aphrodite**, adding a splash of myth and romance to the day.

You don't need any experience to enjoy these tours. Most boats are family-friendly and provide everything you need — from life jackets and shaded areas to snacks, drinks, and snorkeling gear. Some even include a traditional Cypriot lunch onboard, cooked fresh while you sail. Just bring a swimsuit, a towel, sunscreen, and your sense of adventure.

Boat tours run **daily from spring through late autumn**, with more frequent departures in July and August. Tours can last anywhere from **2 hours to a full day**, depending on what you choose. Prices range from **€20 to €50 per person for standard trips**, and **more for private charters** or luxury catamarans. If you're visiting during peak season, it's a good idea to book ahead, either online or at the marina.

Most tours leave in the **morning or early afternoon**, though sunset cruises are also available — and they're magical. Watching the sun dip below the horizon from the middle of the sea, with golden light bouncing off the water, is something you'll remember long after the trip is over.

Whether you want to swim in quiet bays, dance to music on deck, or simply lie back and let the ocean carry you, a coastal cruise is one of those experiences that captures the freedom and beauty of Cyprus perfectly. It's a moment to unplug, breathe in the salt air, and see just how stunning this island truly is — not from the beach, but from the sea.

ACCOMODATION

Hotel

When you're planning your stay in South Cyprus, finding the right hotel can shape your entire experience. The island offers a wide variety of hotels, each offering its own kind of atmosphere, setting, and charm. Whether you're looking for a luxury getaway by the sea, a quiet city stay with everything close by, or a peaceful retreat surrounded by nature, you'll find something that fits both your style and your budget.

If you choose to stay in a hotel near the coast, you'll be waking up to the sound of waves and the scent of the sea. In towns like Paphos, Limassol, and Larnaca, many hotels are within walking distance of beautiful beaches, historic ruins, local markets, and popular restaurants. For example, in Paphos, you can stay just minutes away from the famous Tombs of the Kings and the lively harbor promenade. In Limassol, you'll find hotels nestled between the bustling marina and the charming Old Town, where cobbled streets lead to coffee shops, boutiques, and art galleries. Larnaca gives you the comfort of being close to both the beach and cultural highlights like the Church of Saint Lazarus or the salt lake that's often flocked with flamingos in the winter.

Hotels in these areas are designed to meet all kinds of travel needs. Some are full-service resorts with rooftop pools, spas, and fine dining, while others are small boutique hotels that offer more privacy and personality. Most hotels in the mid to upper price range include daily breakfast, room service, and helpful front desk staff who can assist you with bookings, recommendations, or transportation. Room rates vary depending on the season and location, but during the busy summer months, it's normal for prices to rise. For a mid-range hotel, you can expect to pay anywhere from 75 to 120 euros per night, while luxury hotels may cost well over 200 euros a night in peak season. In quieter months like early spring or late autumn, rates are often significantly lower, and you can find excellent hotels at much more affordable prices.

Many hotels are located close to well-known landmarks, which makes sightseeing easier and more enjoyable. In the heart of Nicosia, staying in a hotel near the old Venetian walls means you can explore both the modern city and its ancient heart without needing a car. In Protaras, hotels near Fig Tree Bay offer direct access to one of the island's most beautiful beaches, and in Ayia Napa, the lively energy of the town center is just a few steps away from many popular hotel options. If you're someone who enjoys walking out the door and being instantly surrounded by culture, history, and food, then choosing a hotel in the middle of town might be the best fit.

But hotels in South Cyprus are not only found in the city. You can also find them in the mountains or tucked into the countryside. These quieter hotels offer fresh air, beautiful landscapes, and a chance to connect with nature. Some are located near hiking trails or ancient monasteries and provide a completely different kind of stay—one that's peaceful, slow-paced, and deeply relaxing. They may not have ocean views, but they often make up for it with breathtaking scenery, homemade breakfasts, and the kind of quiet that helps you truly unwind.

One of the most appreciated aspects of staying in hotels in South Cyprus is the level of hospitality. Staff are usually friendly, warm, and ready to go the extra mile to make your stay more comfortable. From helping with restaurant recommendations to arranging tours or even sharing a bit of local history, they play a big role in making your trip memorable. Many guests leave feeling like they've been welcomed not just into a hotel, but into a small, friendly part of the island's culture.

Booking in advance is recommended, especially during holidays or the summer months when rooms can fill up quickly. If you're visiting during the off-season, you'll often have more flexibility and a wider range of choices. Whether you're after a five-star resort, a stylish boutique hotel, or a clean, simple place to rest after a day of exploring, you'll find hotels across South Cyprus that match your travel rhythm.

The key is to know what kind of experience you want—whether that's sun-soaked days by the pool, sunset walks along the promenade, or quiet evenings under the stars—and choose a place that helps bring that to life. With so many hotels to choose from and such a variety of settings, you'll have no trouble finding one that turns your stay into something special.

Villas

If you're the kind of traveler who loves privacy, space, and the feeling of living like a local, staying in a villa in South Cyprus might be the perfect choice for you. Villas offer a unique kind of freedom that you simply don't get in hotels. From the moment you walk through the doors, everything feels a little more personal. You're not just visiting — you're living here, even if just for a little while.

There's something special about waking up in your own space, brewing a fresh cup of coffee in a quiet kitchen, and stepping out onto a private terrace where the sun is already warming the day. Many villas in South Cyprus come with private pools, gardens, barbecue areas, and sometimes even outdoor dining spaces where you can enjoy long, slow meals under the stars. Whether you're traveling as a couple, with friends, or as a family, the space and comfort of a villa can make your trip feel like a true escape.

You'll find villas scattered all over the island, each offering something a little different. Along the coast, especially in areas like Protaras, Coral Bay, and the hills above Paphos, you'll discover stunning villas perched above the sea or nestled within peaceful olive groves. These locations are close to beaches and town centers, yet offer just enough distance to let you disconnect from the noise. Some villas are even within walking distance to attractions, while others require a short drive — which is worth it for the views and quiet.

In the **Paphos** region, for example, villas near the Coral Bay area place you near the popular beach and close enough to restaurants and shops, but still far enough to enjoy peace and privacy. In **Protaras**, the villas near Fig Tree Bay are ideal for beach lovers, offering easy access to turquoise waters and scenic coastal walks. If you're more interested in mountain views and cooler breezes, you might fall in love with the stone-built villas tucked into the **Troodos Mountains** or nearby villages like **Platres** and **Kakopetria**, where the charm of traditional architecture meets the calm of the countryside.

Prices for villas in South Cyprus vary depending on the season, location, size, and amenities. In the peak summer months, luxury villas with pools and sea views can range from around 180 to 500 euros per night, especially in highly sought-after areas. However, during spring or autumn, those same villas often become more affordable. Smaller or more rustic villas in the countryside can be found at lower prices and still offer an incredibly rewarding experience, especially if you're looking for peace and quiet above anything else.

What makes villas such an attractive choice is the lifestyle they offer. You're not bound by set meal times, you don't need to share space with strangers, and you can truly move at your own pace. You can cook your own meals if you want to, try out local produce from the market, or invite friends over for a sunset dinner by the pool. Everything is more relaxed, more flexible, and more yours. And when you return at the end of a long day exploring, there's no better feeling than stepping into a place that feels like home — even if it's only for a week or two.

Villas are also perfect for travelers who value quiet mornings, space to stretch out, and a sense of comfort that blends well with adventure. With your own kitchen, you can enjoy lazy breakfasts without having to dress up or rush out. You can plan your day in your own time — maybe head to the beach, go on a winery tour, explore an ancient ruin, or just stay in and read while lounging in the sun. That's the beauty of having your own space. You're not a guest following a schedule — you're living your own version of a Cypriot holiday.

Many villas are also ideal for longer stays. If you plan on spending more than a few days in South Cyprus, having a home base that feels cozy and familiar can make your experience much more comfortable. Some villas even include laundry rooms, smart TVs, fast Wi-Fi, and other conveniences that help you settle in with ease.

Whether you're looking to spend your days soaking in the sun with your feet in a pool or you're planning an itinerary full of hikes, beaches, and cultural stops, staying in a villa gives you the space and peace to enjoy it all in your own way. It's an experience that blends comfort with adventure, privacy with convenience, and luxury with the warmth of home. Once you try it, you might find it hard to go back to anything else.

Guest Houses

If you're the type of traveler who values warmth, authenticity, and a little local character over big-brand uniformity, then staying in a guesthouse in South Cyprus might be exactly what you're looking for. Guesthouses offer a completely different experience from hotels or villas. They're usually smaller, more personal, and often family-run. That means you're not just renting a room — you're stepping into someone's home, or at least into a space that has been cared for with that kind of attention.

Guesthouses are scattered across the island, and each one carries its own personality. In coastal areas like Latchi or Pissouri, you'll find whitewashed houses turned into peaceful guest stays, often with a handful of rooms and a simple garden courtyard where you can sip your morning coffee. In the mountain villages like Lefkara, Kalopanayiotis, or Tochni, guesthouses are often built from old stone and timber, beautifully restored to reflect traditional Cypriot architecture. You might find rooms with wooden beams, handmade lace curtains, or small balconies that look out over tiled rooftops and sun-drenched hillsides. These places make you feel connected not just to the island, but to its people and stories.

The price is another appealing part of staying in a guesthouse. Compared to hotels and villas, guesthouses tend to be more budget-friendly, making them a great choice for solo travelers, couples, or anyone planning a longer trip without spending too much. Prices usually start from around 40 or 50 euros per night for a basic room and can go up to about 100 euros for more upgraded, boutique-style guesthouses that include extra touches like organic breakfasts, cozy fireplaces, or in-room kitchens. Many also provide discounts for weekly stays or off-season visits, which is perfect if you want to slow down and truly immerse yourself in your surroundings.

One of the best things about guesthouses is the human connection. In many of them, the owner or host will greet you personally, offer you a welcome drink or snack, and take a few minutes to recommend the best local taverns or the quietest walking paths. These are the kind of tips you won't find in brochures or online guides — the kind that only someone who lives there can offer. They might share stories about the village, point you to the best bakery in town, or explain how to time your visit to a nearby monastery so you can catch a sunset no one else knows about. And because many guesthouses are located in smaller towns or rural areas, you're often encouraged to slow down, listen more, and take in details you might otherwise overlook.

You'll also find that guesthouses attract a different kind of traveler. People who stay in these places often come with a curiosity about culture, history, and daily life in Cyprus. That means it's not unusual to end up sharing a conversation over breakfast with other guests from all over the world, swapping travel stories, or finding common ground in a shared appreciation for the quiet beauty of the island.

Even though guesthouses are usually simple, that doesn't mean they lack comfort. Many now blend traditional design with modern amenities like Wi-Fi, air conditioning, and en suite bathrooms. You get the charm of the old world with the conveniences of the new, which makes the experience all the more pleasant. And if you're visiting during winter, you'll find that some of the mountain guesthouses even offer wood-burning stoves or underfloor heating to keep things cozy.

Another benefit of staying in a guesthouse is the connection to nature and the rhythms of local life. You might hear the church bell ring softly in the morning, smell fresh bread baking down the road, or see village children playing in the square as you sip coffee from a small terrace. It's these little moments that make your stay unforgettable. You're not just passing through; you're part of it, even if only for a few days.

Whether you're exploring the hills of Troodos, cycling through vineyards, or simply watching the sky change colors over a sleepy village, a guesthouse can become a peaceful, grounding part of your journey. It's where comfort meets culture, and where strangers become hosts, and sometimes even friends. If what you're looking for is more than just a place to sleep, a guesthouse will give you a place to feel something real — and that's what great travel is all about.

Holiday Apartments

Choosing to stay in a holiday apartment in South Cyprus is one of the smartest ways to enjoy both freedom and comfort while getting a more local feel for the island. It's a perfect option for travelers who want something in between a hotel and a private villa — a place that feels like home, but still has the flexibility and accessibility to help you explore with ease. Whether you're here for a few days or a few weeks, an apartment gives you the room to breathe, cook, relax, and live on your own schedule.

Apartments are especially popular in the coastal cities like Larnaca, Limassol, and Paphos. In these places, you can easily find modern holiday flats just steps away from the beach, tucked behind lively town squares, or perched on quiet side streets where you can wake up to the sound of morning church bells or smell of fresh bread from the bakery down the road. You get the convenience of having restaurants, shops, and transportation all nearby, while still having your own kitchen, living room, and sometimes even a balcony with sea views or garden corners.

If you're traveling with family, a holiday apartment makes it much easier to keep everyone comfortable. You can make your own meals, do your laundry, and settle in without relying on hotel schedules. This kind of setup is also perfect for groups of friends or couples who enjoy space and privacy without the price tag of a villa. Many apartments in tourist-favorite towns are within walking distance to landmarks, beaches, and cultural attractions. For example, in Paphos, you might stay just a ten-minute walk from the harbor while also being near the Archaeological Park. In Limassol, it's common to find apartments just off the marina or around the Old Town, close to the medieval castle and nightlife. Larnaca's apartments often overlook the palm-lined Finikoudes promenade or sit quietly a few streets behind it.

In terms of price, holiday apartments offer great value, especially if you're staying for more than a few nights. You'll find small studio apartments starting around 50 to 70 euros per night in the off-season, while larger two- or three-bedroom places near the beach can range from 90 to 150 euros or more, depending on the time of year. Summer tends to be more expensive, especially in July and August, but booking ahead often helps you secure better deals. And if you're visiting during spring or late autumn, prices tend to drop, making it easier to stretch your budget further.

One of the biggest perks of staying in an apartment is the chance to live like a local. You can shop at nearby markets, cook with Cypriot ingredients, and enjoy slow, easy mornings without the rush of hotel check-in desks or breakfast deadlines. It's a more laid-back way to travel, and you might find yourself slipping into a slower, more peaceful rhythm without even trying. The experience feels more intimate, more grounded, and for many travelers, far more memorable.

Most holiday apartments are well-equipped, offering air conditioning, Wi-Fi, fully fitted kitchens, and washing machines. Some even come with extras like rooftop terraces, shared pools, or underground parking — especially in newer apartment complexes. You'll usually be greeted by a host or local manager who can give you tips about the area, help you with check-in, and answer any questions during your stay. This kind of personal touch can make a big difference when you're visiting a place for the first time.

If you're planning to explore different parts of the island, holiday apartments can also be a great base. Spend a few days in one city, then move to another, all while enjoying the consistency of your own kitchen and space. Or choose one apartment in a central location and take day trips to the mountains, beaches, and historic villages — returning each evening to a familiar, comfortable space.

For travelers who value independence, local charm, and good value, holiday apartments are a smart and satisfying choice. They allow you to settle in, spread out, and enjoy Cyprus in a way that feels both relaxed and real. Whether you're here to discover the history, soak up the sun, or simply escape your usual routine, staying in a holiday apartment helps you do it all at your own pace.

PRACTICAL INFORMATION

Local Etiquette and Customs

When you visit South Cyprus, you're not just stepping into a sunny travel destination — you're entering a place with deep cultural roots, proud traditions, and a warm, welcoming way of life. Understanding a bit about the local etiquette and customs before you arrive can help you feel more at home, show respect to the people around you, and make your travel experience even more rewarding. You'll notice quickly that Cypriots are incredibly friendly and hospitable, and when you return that kindness with thoughtfulness and awareness, your time here will feel even more meaningful.

First, let's talk about greetings. In most situations, a simple "hello" or "yiá sou" (which means hi in Greek) goes a long way. If someone greets you with a smile and a handshake, it's polite to return it the same way. When entering a shop, a café, or even a small office, it's normal to acknowledge the people there with a friendly nod or short greeting. It may seem small, but these gestures are part of daily life, and people really appreciate them. If you're meeting someone older, it's respectful to address them with a bit more formality, especially in village settings.

Cypriot hospitality is something you'll likely experience right away. Whether you're staying in a guesthouse, visiting a winery, or simply chatting with a local at a market, don't be surprised if someone offers you a coffee, a sweet, or even a seat at their table. Accepting these small gestures shows appreciation and often leads to great conversations. Saying "efcharistó" (thank you) is a simple way to show your gratitude, and people will notice the effort.

Dress codes in Cyprus are generally relaxed, especially at the beach or in touristy areas. But when you visit monasteries, churches, or traditional villages, it's important to dress modestly. That means covering your shoulders and wearing something that goes below the knees. If you're not dressed appropriately, some religious sites may ask you to wrap a shawl or scarf over your clothes, which they often provide at the entrance. Being respectful in sacred spaces helps preserve the dignity of places that hold real meaning for locals.

Dining customs also have their own rhythm. If you're invited to someone's home for a meal — which is not uncommon here — it's polite to bring a small gift, like a dessert or a bottle of wine. When eating out, you'll often find that meals are served slowly and enjoyed at a leisurely pace. It's not unusual for dinners to stretch for hours, especially when meze is involved. Nobody's in a rush, and that's part of the charm. Also, don't expect your check to arrive the moment you finish eating — in Cyprus, meals are meant to be enjoyed without pressure, and asking for the bill is completely normal when you're ready.

You might also notice that family plays a huge role in daily life. Sunday is a day when many locals gather for big family lunches, often in a relative's home or a favorite tavern. You'll see multi-generational groups laughing, sharing food, and spending real time together. It's a beautiful reminder of how important relationships are here, and it's something that often makes travelers slow down and reflect on their own pace of life.

Public behavior in Cyprus is generally relaxed, but it's best to avoid loud or overly expressive behavior in quiet areas or religious spaces. Drinking in moderation is part of the social culture, but being visibly intoxicated in public — especially away from nightlife areas — can be frowned upon. Showing respect in how you behave, dress, and speak goes a long way here, and locals tend to be very patient and generous toward visitors who make an effort to be polite.

If you're driving around the island, especially in villages or more residential areas, it's helpful to know that Cypriots are courteous drivers but can be quite relaxed about certain rules — sometimes in ways that feel unfamiliar. Still, being patient, following signs, and giving a friendly wave when someone lets you pass is always appreciated. Parking near someone's home or business is usually fine, as long as you're not blocking their entrance or driveway.

Understanding the basics of local customs also helps when visiting places like markets, bakeries, or local festivals. It's okay to ask questions, taste things before you buy, and take your time browsing. People are often happy to explain what something is, where it's from, or how it's made. Just show interest, be kind, and you'll find that conversations often open doors you didn't expect — both literally and figuratively.

In the end, you don't need to be perfect. Cypriots don't expect you to know every cultural detail. What they do appreciate is sincerity, kindness, and a willingness to learn. When you travel with curiosity and respect, you'll find that the island opens up to you in the most genuine and heartwarming ways. And before you know it, you won't just feel like a visitor — you'll feel like a welcome guest.

Accessibility for Disabled Travelers

Traveling through South Cyprus can be a fulfilling and enriching experience, and it's becoming more inclusive every year for travelers with disabilities. If you have mobility challenges, use a wheelchair, or rely on accessible services to navigate a new place, you'll find that many areas are slowly adapting to better meet your needs. While there's still room for improvement in certain rural and older parts of the island, the good news is that most major cities, public spaces, and many tourist attractions are making efforts to be more accessible.

When you arrive at Larnaca or Paphos International Airport, you'll notice that accessibility is taken seriously. Both airports provide assistance services from the moment you land, with elevators, accessible restrooms, and pathways that make moving through terminals smoother. If you need help, staff can provide assistance on arrival and departure — just make sure to let your airline know ahead of time so arrangements are in place. Accessible taxis are also available, though they should be booked in advance to avoid long waits.

As you explore the cities, you'll find that many of the sidewalks in places like Limassol, Larnaca, and Paphos have ramps and dropped curbs, though the condition and width of some sidewalks can vary. The newer parts of these cities — especially near the seafront promenades — are much easier to navigate with wheelchairs or mobility scooters. You'll also come across modern cafés and restaurants with step-free entrances and wide interior spaces. Staff are usually more than willing to help if you need a hand with doors or seating.

Public transportation is improving in terms of accessibility. Most buses in major urban areas are equipped with low floors and ramps, and drivers are trained to assist passengers with special needs. You can board these buses with a wheelchair, though it's still a good idea to double-check specific routes or call ahead if you're unsure. Bus companies like Cyprus Public Transport also provide information online about which buses are accessible. Taxis that are specially adapted for wheelchairs can be arranged through a few companies, though they tend to be more available in the larger cities than in remote villages.

When it comes to places of interest, more and more cultural and historical sites are becoming accessible. The Cyprus Museum in Nicosia and the Paphos Archaeological Park both offer wheelchair access to several areas, with ramps, wide paths, and helpful signage. You'll also find that many modern hotels — particularly the higher-end ones — are equipped with accessible rooms that include roll-in showers, wider doorways, and elevator access. Some even have beach wheelchairs available, especially in areas like Ayia Napa and Limassol, where designated accessible beaches provide pathways across the sand, floating beach wheelchairs, and shaded lounging areas.

Even though traditional villages and mountain paths might still present a challenge, many rural accommodations and agrotourism guesthouses are working to include step-free entrances and accessible bathrooms. If you plan to visit these areas, it's always a good idea to reach out ahead of time to ask specific questions about what they offer. Hosts are usually eager to help and may even be able to make temporary adjustments for your comfort.

Some wellness centers and spas also include accessible facilities, particularly in resort areas. Whether you're hoping to enjoy a massage, hydrotherapy pool, or just relax in a peaceful setting, you can find places that are happy to accommodate your needs with dignity and care. Beaches like Finikoudes in Larnaca and Dasoudi in Limassol offer excellent accessibility, making it easier to enjoy the coast without stress.

The most important thing to remember is that people in Cyprus are generally very helpful. Even when infrastructure isn't perfect, locals are often willing to go the extra mile to assist — whether that means helping you board a bus, adjusting a restaurant table, or offering a closer parking spot. With a bit of planning and flexibility, you can enjoy everything from the island's rich history and natural beauty to its lively food scene and cultural experiences.

Sustainable Travel Tips

When you come to South Cyprus, you'll quickly fall in love with its natural beauty — the clear blue waters, the forested hills, the sleepy mountain villages, and the sun-drenched coastlines. But as more people discover this incredible place, the need to travel responsibly becomes even more important. Making small, thoughtful choices as you explore can help protect this island for generations to come, and the good news is that sustainable travel here isn't complicated — it just means being a little more mindful with how you move, where you stay, what you consume, and how you treat the environment around you.

One of the easiest ways to lower your impact is to support local businesses. When you eat at a family-owned taverna, buy handmade crafts in a village, or stay in a locally-run guesthouse, your money goes directly into the community. It helps keep traditions alive, strengthens small economies, and encourages people to keep sharing their culture and knowledge. You'll also notice that the experience is more personal and memorable. Locals love to share stories, recommend hidden spots, and welcome you as more than just a tourist. It's a more rewarding way to travel — not just for you, but for the people who live here.

South Cyprus has a public bus system that's improving every year, especially in major towns like Larnaca, Limassol, and Nicosia. Using public transport when you can, or even renting a bike in flatter areas, reduces traffic and cuts down on emissions. If you're planning to rent a car, consider choosing a fuel-efficient model or sharing rides with other travelers when possible. Driving carefully and sticking to marked roads also helps preserve the countryside, especially in remote areas like the Akamas Peninsula or the Troodos mountains, where nature is more fragile.

You'll find that tap water is generally safe to drink in most parts of the island, so bringing a reusable water bottle can save money and cut down on plastic waste. The same goes for reusable shopping bags and containers, especially if you're picking up snacks from local bakeries or shopping at the weekly markets. Many coastal towns are making efforts to reduce single-use plastics, and you can do your part just by being prepared.

When you visit beaches, trails, and historic sites, it's always good to leave things as you found them — or even better. Take your trash with you, respect signs and protected areas, and avoid touching ancient ruins or removing shells, stones, or flowers. These things may seem small, but they help preserve the character and health of the places you're enjoying. Even a quiet forest path or a secluded beach has its own balance, and your care keeps that balance intact.

If you're interested in deeper eco-experiences, consider staying at an agrotourism lodge or eco-village, especially in the countryside. These places often grow their own food, use solar power, and teach you about local farming or winemaking traditions. It's a peaceful, inspiring way to connect with nature and the community at the same time. You can find eco-lodges tucked away in the hills, near vineyards, or close to trails — and many of them are as comfortable and stylish as any modern hotel.

Being a responsible traveler doesn't mean you have to give up fun or comfort. It just means paying attention to how your trip affects the island and choosing options that give something back. Whether you're hiking a gorge, sunbathing at the beach, or shopping for souvenirs, there's always a more conscious way to do it. And as you move through Cyprus, you'll feel proud knowing that your journey is helping to protect the places you love for the next person who comes along.

Shopping Hours and Public Holidays

As you explore South Cyprus, you'll find plenty of chances to shop — whether you're wandering through a local market, stepping into a charming little boutique, or stocking up on snacks and souvenirs in a city center. But to make the most of your time and avoid any surprises, it helps to know how shopping hours usually work here, as well as when public holidays might change your plans.

Shopping in Cyprus doesn't follow a strict one-size-fits-all schedule. Instead, opening hours often vary depending on the type of shop, its location, and even the season. In the bigger towns and tourist areas like Limassol, Larnaca, Paphos, and Nicosia, you'll notice that larger stores and shopping malls usually open around 9 or 10 in the morning and stay open until about 8 or 9 in the evening. These places are often open Monday through Saturday, and many stay open on Sundays too, especially during the summer months when tourists are out in full force.

Smaller, independent shops — particularly those in villages or more residential neighborhoods — tend to follow a more traditional rhythm. They might open in the morning, close for a few hours in the early afternoon, and then reopen later in the day. That midday break usually happens between 1 and 4 p.m., especially during the hotter months, and it's part of the slower, relaxed pace of life here. If you're planning to visit a bakery, butcher, or corner shop, it's best to go either before noon or after 4 to be safe. And on Wednesdays and Saturday afternoons, many smaller stores close early and don't reopen until the next day.

When it comes to public holidays, things slow down even more. Cyprus observes a mix of national and religious holidays, and on these days, many businesses shut their doors entirely — including government offices, banks, and most stores. On big holidays like Easter Sunday, Christmas Day, and August 15th (Assumption

Day), even supermarkets and petrol stations may operate on reduced hours or close completely. Other key holidays include Green Monday (usually in March), Greek Independence Day on March 25th, Labour Day on May 1st, and Cyprus Independence Day on October 1st. During these times, you'll find that locals spend time with family, attend church services, or join in parades and celebrations.

Some holidays move around each year depending on the Orthodox Christian calendar, especially Easter, which is one of the most important times of the year in Cyprus. The week leading up to Easter Sunday can be busy with preparations and services, and many businesses may change their hours, so it's a good idea to plan ahead. That said, even on holidays, you'll still find a few restaurants, cafés, and small minimarkets open — particularly in tourist areas where the pace never fully stops.

If you're ever unsure whether something will be open, a quick chat with a hotel receptionist, local host, or shopkeeper will usually clear things up. People are happy to help and often have the most up-to-date information, especially for village areas where schedules can change based on tradition or season.

Being aware of local shopping habits and holiday schedules means you can enjoy your time more, avoid closed doors, and maybe even join in on a celebration or two. It's just another way to experience the island not just as a visitor, but as someone moving in step with the real rhythm of life here.

CONCLUSION

And just like that, we've come to the end of this travel guide — but your journey through South Cyprus is only just beginning.

By now, you've had a taste of everything this beautiful island has to offer. You've wandered through cobbled mountain villages and stood in awe before ancient churches. You've lounged on beaches where the sea shimmers like glass, danced under the stars in lively city squares, and tasted flavors that linger long after the last bite. Maybe you've planned your route to hike a gorge or sail along the coast, sip wine among the vineyards, or slow down in a quiet spa tucked between the hills.

The goal of this book was never just to point you from one landmark to another. It was to show you what it really feels like to be here — to soak up the light, the smells, the sounds, and the stories that live in every corner of this island. Whether you're a first-time visitor or someone who's returning for the second, third, or tenth time, South Cyprus always has something new to show you — not just a place, but a feeling.

This guide is meant to be your companion, not your commander. Take the suggestions, the tips, the experiences, and make them your own. Let your curiosity guide you. Let spontaneity sneak in when it wants to. The best memories are often made when you wander down a street you hadn't planned to, or say yes to something you've never tried before. Whether it's striking up a conversation with a local at a market, finding a hidden cove, or hearing music drifting from a quiet taverna, Cyprus rewards those who travel with an open heart.

More than anything, I hope this guide helped you feel a little more confident, a little more excited, and a little more prepared to explore — without the stress of uncertainty or the fear of missing out. Every location, every activity, every recommendation here was chosen with love and based on real experiences. I wanted you to feel like a friend had handed you a map, circled the best spots, and whispered, "Don't skip this part."

But now, it's your turn. Your time to walk the paths, taste the dishes, breathe the fresh mountain air, dive into the blue, and write your own story here. Maybe you'll fall in love with the stillness of a small village or the buzz of a seaside city. Maybe you'll come back home with sand in your shoes, stories in your pockets, and plans to return. Or maybe — just maybe — you'll never want to leave.

Whatever your story becomes, I hope South Cyprus becomes a part of it — and I hope this book helped you start that chapter.

So go ahead. The island is waiting for you.

Printed in Dunstable, United Kingdom